EXPLORING
psychology

for AS Level AQA 'A'

study and
revision guide

Julia Russell
Jean-Marc Lawton

OXFORD
UNIVERSITY PRESS

Great Clarendon Street, Oxford OX2 6DP

Oxford University Press is a department of the University of Oxford.
It furthers the University's objective of excellence in research, scholarship, and education by publishing worldwide in

Oxford   New York

Auckland   Cape Town   Dar es Salaam   Hong Kong   Karachi   Kuala Lumpur
Madrid   Melbourne   Mexico City   Nairobi   New Delhi   Shanghai   Taipei   Toronto

With offices in
Argentina   Austria   Brazil   Chile   Czech Republic   France   Greece   Guatemala
Hungary   Italy   Japan   Poland   Portugal   Singapore   South Korea   Switzerland
Thailand   Turkey   Ukraine   Vietnam

Oxford is a registered trade mark of Oxford University Press in the UK and in certain other countries

British Library Cataloguing in Publication Data

Data available

ISBN 978 1 85008 540 9

FD5409

10 9 8 7 6 5 4 3 2 1

Printed by Bell and Bain

Paper used in the production of this book is a natural, recyclable product made from wood grown in sustainable forests. The manufacturing process conforms to the environmental regulations of the country of origin.

Acknowledgements

The publisher and authors would like to thank the following for their permission to reproduce photographs and other copyright material:
aleksandar kamasi/Fotolia, p68; Allen Johnson/iStockphoto, p22; coutesy of Julia Russell, p26, 27, 58, 110; Doctor Kan/Fotolia, p73; Dr Walter Boot, PhD at Florida State University, p46; drx/Fotolia, p59; Elena Galach'yants/Fotolia, p75; elenarostunova/Fotolia, p75; emily2k/Fotolia; Fotolia, p109; Harry Venning, p11; javarman/Fotolia; Jim DeLillo/iStockphoto, p19; Laurence Gough/123rf, p18; Leah Anne Thompson/123rf, p91; courtesy of the National Archives, p85: Norbert Martin/Fotolia; Oleksandr/Fotolia; Pavel Losevsky/Fotolia, p34; Robert Churchill/iStockphoto, p90; Sara Robinson/Fotolia, p82; SciencePhotoLibrary, p20; Sergey Tokarev/Fotolia; Tomasz Trojanowski/Fotolia, p35; wikimedia commons, p101,109; WILLSIE/iStockphoto, p25; Yuri Arcurs/iStockphoto, p25

Every effort has been made to contact copyright holders of material reproduced in this book. If notified, the publishers will be pleased to rectify any errors or omissions at the earliest opportunity.

Project Management: Rick Jackman (Jackman Publishing Solutions Ltd)
Editor: Cathy Hurren
Concept design: Patricia Briggs
Text layout: Nigel Harriss
Cover design: Patricia Briggs
Cover image: James Cant/Getty Images

Thank you to Cathy who has been absolutely brilliant; to Jean-Marc for his excellent contribution and to Rick whose unstinting support is so much appreciated.

Dedication

To Dad, with love.

Contents

Chapter 4 – Biological Psychology

Chapter 5 – Social Psychology

Chapter 6 – Individual Differences

Chapter 7 – Studying and Revising

Glossary

Introduction

Starting an AS-level course presents new challenges. The work is harder than at GCSE, there is much more of it, it is tested in different and more demanding ways and you as a student are expected to be a more independent learner. This book aims to help you to cope with these challenges. It provides ideas for improving your understanding and performance during your course, as well as guidance on what and how to revise in anticipation of the examinations.

Each of the main chapters covers one of the topics from Units 1 and 2 of the AQA–A AS in Psychology course. Each aspect of the specification is covered, providing an outline of what is required, the terms you should know and a detailed exploration of the concepts, theories, studies and research methods required. Within this coverage, descriptions, evaluations and applications are provided in separate boxes. This allows you to pick out just the information you need, which is ideal for reference during your course or to find key points when you are revising. The layout follows the same basic structure as the specification itself and the accompanying Folens student's textbook, *Exploring Psychology for AS Level AQA 'A'*, but this book can be used effectively with any other text. In addition, each chapter includes features to help you to study and revise well. These include:

- Study notes – these draw your attention to strategies for learning, ways to improve your understanding and important aspects of examination technique.
- Revision notes – these suggest ideas to help you to remember key points and to avoid frequent pitfalls.
- Thinking psychologically boxes – these give you the opportunity to explore your understanding and apply your knowledge.
- Exam focus questions – these look at student answers to examination-style questions through the eyes of an examiner, giving a commentary on the answers and advice on what the student could have done to improve them.

This book has been written with input and advice from a senior examiner for AS-level Psychology, so you can be certain that the examiner's advice throughout will guide you in the right direction.

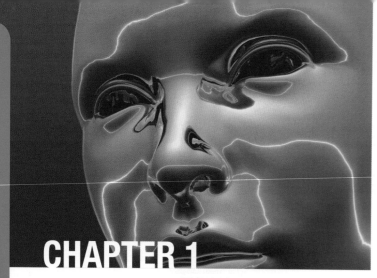

CHAPTER 1
Cognitive Psychology

1.1 An Introduction to Cognitive Psychology

YOU NEED TO:

know what these terms mean:

- cognitive psychology
- memory
- encoding
- storage
- capacity

describe and evaluate:

- the multi-store model
- the working memory model

understand and apply techniques for improving memory:

- using cues
- using mnemonics

understand and apply your knowledge about factors affecting eyewitness testimony, including:

- the effect of anxiety
- the effect of age
- the effect of misleading questions
- the cognitive interview and its benefits

KEY TERMS

cognitive psychology focuses on receiving, changing, storing and using information. It includes the processes of attention, perception, memory, decision-making and language

encoding the form of representation that is used to hold information in memory, e.g. visual (sight-based), acoustic (sound-based) or semantic (meaning-based)

capacity the maximum amount of information that can be held in a memory store at one time, i.e. how much fits in before the store is full

duration how long information can be held in memory for, i.e. the length of storage over time

memory the encoding and storage of information that is later retrieved

cognitive interview a technique used to improve accuracy for testimonies gained from witnesses which aims to recreate internal and environmental cues for the witness, to get them to report information in different orders and from different perspectives, and to report incomplete or irrelevant details

1.2 The Multi-Store Model

The multi-store model

Within **cognitive psychology**, explanations help us to understand how we process information. Atkinson & Shiffrin (1968) produced a model which attempted to explain why we remember some things better than others. They suggested that there are different 'stores'. These differ in terms of:

- how they represent information (**encoding**)
- how much they store (**capacity**)
- how long information is held (**duration**).

These stores are in white boxes in Figure 1.1.

The multi-store model (MSM) of **memory** also proposes '**control processes**', which are the ways in which information is dealt with (in dark green in Figure 1.1).

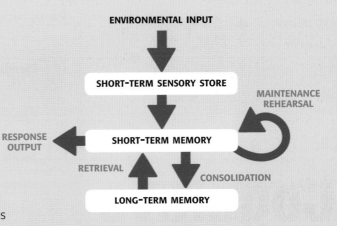

Figure 1.1 The multi-store model.

Short-term sensory store

Information from each of the senses has its own **short-term sensory store** (STSS). In each store information is *encoded* in a **modality specific** way because they deal with information from one sense. The STSS for vision is the **iconic store** and the one for sound is the **echoic store**.

Sperling (1960) showed that the iconic store has a very limited *duration* (a few seconds or less) and a moderate *capacity*. Participants who saw a matrix of 12 letters could recall about as much from the whole matrix as they could from just one row. This suggests that the participants had, for just a few milliseconds, a clear memory of the whole matrix but that the memory faded quickly. Sperling found that an iconic memory lasts about 0.5 seconds.

In terms of encoding, the echoic store is also modality specific, representing information acoustically. Its duration is also time-limited. Treisman (1964) used a shadowing task (listening to a different message in each ear and repeating only one) to show that the duration of the echoic store was about two seconds. If the delay between the messages was less than this the participants didn't notice the difference.

V	**M**	**G**	**U**
P	**F**	**O**	**B**
A	**L**	**X**	**S**

Figure 1.2 According to Sperling (1960) you can only remember the whole matrix for about half a second before it fades from the iconic store.

Study note

Think:
- icons are visual tags on the computer (the iconic store is visual)
- echoes are sounds (the echoic store is sound-based)

Short-term memory

The **short-term memory** (STM) has a short *duration* – about 18 seconds according to Peterson & Peterson (1959). They measured how well participants retained nonsense trigrams, e.g. XPF, in STM when **rehearsal** was prevented for differing lengths of time. The longer the delay before recall was allowed, the worse the participants' memory for the trigrams. Participants were prevented from rehearsing the trigrams by being asked to count backwards; this causes **interference**, causing material in STM to be lost. Without interference, rehearsal transfers information to the long-term memory.

According to Miller (1956) the STM also has a limited *capacity* of approximately 7±2 items or 'chunks', i.e. it gets 'full' easily. Taking in more information pushes older items out, i.e. it causes **displacement**. A **chunk** is information which has been grouped together into a single unit although the size of a chunk can vary. Chunking related information (treating multiple items as one) can therefore reduce displacement.

The MSM suggests that information in STM is *encoded* **acoustically**, that is it uses a sound-based code. This explains why we tend to make errors with similar sounding items on immediate recall tasks.

E O I
H
L V S
G O C
Y L P O Y

Figure 1.3 This set of letters can easily be stored in STM even though there are many more than 7±2 items. How? (Answer on page 4.)

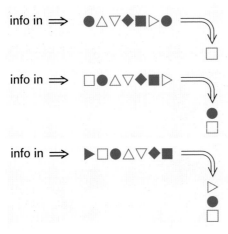

info in ⟹ ●△▽◆■▷●

info in ⟹ □●△▽◆■▷

info in ⟹ ▶□●△▽◆■

Figure 1.4 Displacement of items in STM happens because it has a limited capacity.

(Answer to Figure 1.3 on page 3 – the letters can be chunked into three words: I love psychology.)

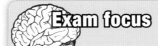

Exam focus

Pair up each memory store on the left with **one** statement on the right.

(3 marks)

1. Encoding	a) The form used to represent information in a memory store.
2. Capacity	b) The maximum amount of information that can be held in a memory store.
3. Duration	c) How long a memory can last for.

Examiner commentary

Exam papers usually start with an easy question to get you going. Be careful that you don't rush it and misread a simple statement. (Answers: the correct answers here happen to match straight across. Sometimes answers are more obvious than they look!)

Long-term memory

Long-term memories have a *duration* of minutes to years and can last a lifetime, although we do forget things from long-term memory (LTM) too. Linton (1975) tested herself on events she recorded in a daily diary. She could recall 70 per cent of events with the aid of a single keyword up to seven years later. This study demonstrates the long duration, and also shows the enormous *capacity*, of LTM as her diaries contained about 11,000 items!

Bahrick (1984) demonstrated the duration of LTM by showing that people who had been taught Spanish up to 50 years before his study could still remember a lot. The fastest forgetting occurred in the first three years or so after which the memories formed a 'permastore', that is, they stayed relatively constant.

'Do you remember when we chased Mr McGregor's cat along here?'

Figure 1.6

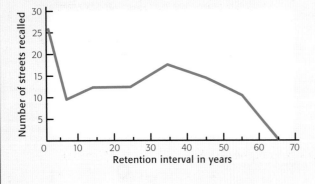

Figure 1.5 Schmidt *et al.* (2000) tested very long-term recall of incidentally (not deliberately) learned street names from childhood and showed, like Bahrick, that although details are lost at first, people still remember well even decades later.

Thinking psychologically

Sachs (1967) showed that LTM uses **semantic** *encoding*. She read participants simple sentences embedded in short paragraphs. Later she presented them with sentences that had been changed either in terms of meaning or in terms of structure. For example, the original sentence, 'The founding fathers considered owning slaves to be immoral' might be changed to, 'The founding fathers considered owning slaves to be moral' which would be spotted, but 'The founding fathers thought owning slaves to be immoral' would not. Why?

Figure 1.7 When recalling the central sentence from LTM, participants would recognise the right-hand option as different, but not the one on the left.

Revision note

It's easy to remember the duration of the different stores; it's in the name:
- **short**-term sensory store
- **short**-term memory
- **long**-term memory.

Hidden in there too is a clue to the capacity (think 'S' for small and 'L' for large):
- S̲TSS • S̲TM • L̲TM.

There's even a hint for encoding:
- STS̲S̲: S̲ight and S̲ound
  (i.e. encoding is specific to each sense)
- L̲T̲M̲: L̲inked T̲o M̲eaning
  (i.e. meaning-based encoding).

Separating STM and LTM

Baddeley (1966) found that although similar sounding words were muddled on immediate recall (because STM uses an acoustic code), with delayed recall more errors were made on words with similar meanings (because LTM uses semantic encoding).

A serial position task presents participants with items to learn in order. Murdock (1962) used this technique with word lists and found that recall for the early and late items was much better than for items in the middle. This suggests that LTM and STM are different memory stores. Items at the beginning of the list were well recalled because they were encoded longest ago so had been rehearsed and transferred to LTM (the **primacy effect**). The middle items were pushed out of STM by listening to the end of the list so were not rehearsed and the items at the end were still in STM (the **recency effect**).

Glanzer & Cunitz (1966) showed that the primacy and recency effects were separate from each other. With a 30-second interference task before recall, the items in STM could not be rehearsed so were forgotten and the recency effect (but not the primacy effect) was lost.

Evidence from people with **amnesia** also shows that STM and LTM are separate. Scoville & Milner (1957) found that the patient HM could make few new long-term memories but his short-term memory was relatively normal.

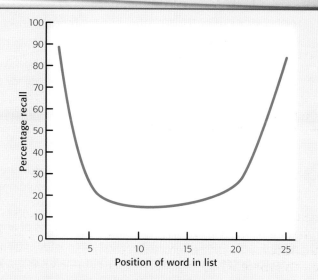

Figure 1.8 A serial position curve.

Thinking psychologically

Murdock (1962) also showed that if the word list was presented very quickly, the primacy effect was reduced without affecting the recency effect. Why?

Draw serial position curves that show the results of fast and slow presentation of words.

Exam focus

Indicate whether each statement below is true or false by ticking **one** box only on each line. *(3 marks)*

	True	False
1. The sensory memory for vision encodes information by how it looks.		
2. Short-term memory has an unlimited capacity.		
3. Long-term memory is mainly semantic.		

Examiner commentary

This is another question style that can be used to start a paper. Make sure that you follow the rubric (the instructions for the question) and only tick as many boxes as you have been asked to. (Answers: 1 True, 2 False, 3 True.)

1.3 Evaluating the Multi-Store Model

Strengths of the multi-store model

+ *Evidence* from well-controlled laboratory experiments illustrates the features of each of the stores in the MSM, such as:
- Sperling (1960) – very short duration but fairly large capacity of the iconic store
- Peterson & Peterson (1959) – STM duration of less than 30 seconds
- Sachs (1967) – semantic encoding in LTM.

+ Laboratory experiments have also shown that STM and LTM are different, e.g.:
- Baddeley (1966) – acoustic encoding in STM but semantic in LTM
- Glanzer & Cunitz (1966) – the primacy-recency effect and loss of the recency effect if recall is delayed because information in STM is displaced.

+ Brain scanning, which is a highly reliable technique, was used by Wiswede *et al.* (2007) to show that different brain areas are active during the primacy and recency effects, showing them to be separate processes.

+ Conners *et al.* (2000) found that participants with Prader-Willi syndrome (which affects memory) had relatively good LTM but poor STM compared to those without the syndrome.

+ Case studies of amnesics such as HM (Scoville & Milner, 1957) support the distinction between STM and LTM as HM could not make new LTMs but his STM still functioned.

+ The MSM also has *relevance* to real life in terms of applications, for example, in avoiding acoustic interference when encoding new material – so try not to have the radio on when you are doing your homework!

Revision note

To remember the different ways that you can evaluate theories – think SWEAR (Strengths, Weaknesses: Evidence, Alternatives, Relevance).

Weaknesses of the multi-store model

− Some *evidence* suggests that STM can encode by meaning, as well as acoustically, e.g. Forde & Humphreys (2002) showed that the amnesic patient FK made fewer pronunciation errors when recalling words he had known before becoming amnesic than on 'new' words, suggesting that if he understood a word this helped him to say it.

− When we perform two similar tasks using STM they interfere but two dissimilar tasks, e.g. visual and auditory ones, don't. This suggests that STM has separate systems for different modalities. Seitz & Schumann-Hengsteler (2000) supported this by showing that doing sums was more easily disrupted by a visual than a sound-based distraction.

− The working memory model is an *alternative* explanation suggesting that there are several different short-term stores, which accounts for findings about task interference that the MSM cannot explain.

− There are also *alternative* ways to consider LTM as it seems to have several types of storage. Declarative memories are about facts and events in contrast to procedural memories for physical skills. The amnesic patient HM, who could learn new physical tasks but not new facts, illustrates this distinction. Semantic memories are of general facts whereas episodic memories relate to personal facts. Facundo *et al.* (2001) showed that the amnesic patient RG could recall procedural and semantic memories, but not episodic ones.

 **Exam focus**

One strength of the multi-store model is that it can account for why amnesic patients experience problems with some types of memory, but not others. How does the multi-store model explain this?
(3 marks)

Jo's answer:

The MSM says we have 3 memory stores so one could be defunct & the others OK. ①

Examiner commentary

This is essentially the right idea but doesn't explain why it is important so only earns one mark. Jo needed to say **how** this explains the differences, e.g. because the STM might function normally but new LTMs cannot be formed, as was the case for HM.

1.4 The Working Memory Model

The working memory model

The **working memory model** (WMM) suggests that the 'temporary' or short-term memory has several subunits. Baddeley & Hitch (1974) initially proposed three subunits: a **central executive** (CE) which takes information in from the senses and sorts it before passing the right kinds of information to two slave units; these are the **phonological loop** (PL) for sound-based items (including speech) and the **visuo-spatial sketch** (or **scratch**) **pad** (VSSP) for visual and spatial information.

The phonological loop

This store uses a sound-based code and has a duration of 2–3 seconds which can be increased with rehearsal. As repetition of items takes time the PL is also time-limited; this explains why similar-sounding items get muddled – because acoustic coding means that even visual items, once represented by sounds, can become confused. It accounts for why a list of short words is remembered better than a list of long words – it takes longer to say long words 'in your head', so they will start to decay sooner than short words. It also explains why verbal and subvocal repetition reduces recall. An interference task like repeating 'the, the, the' occupies the PL so will also prevent rehearsal and reduce recall.

The visuo-spatial sketch pad

Baddeley *et al.* (1973) studied the effect of different kinds of rehearsal on a spatial task. Participants were given either visual or verbal instructions to remember. When also asked to follow a moving light (a spatial task) they found it more difficult to do alongside visual compared to verbal rehearsal; if both tasks use the VSSP performance is affected but if they use separate slave units it is not.

The central executive

The CE is the 'control unit' in working memory and can use any form of encoding. When it receives information (from the senses or from LTM) it sends it to either the PL or the VSSP. It organises working memory by selectively attending to some sources of information rather than others, by switching between sources of input and by dividing attention between different tasks.

As the CE is responsible for resource allocation (receiving information and deciding which slave unit it will go to) it should be under greater pressure when we are doing two tasks at once. In a test placing demands on both processing and memory span, the strain on the CE should be more obvious in people with smaller memory spans as the CE will have a harder job allocating resources. Daneman & Carpenter (1980, 1983) gave participants sentences to read and asked them to recall the last word from each. Participants who recalled the final words more accurately (so had the biggest working memory spans) also had better understanding of the sentences suggesting that their processing was also more effective.

Visuo-spatial sketch pad

Central executive

Phonological loop

Figure 1.9 The working memory model (Baddeley & Hitch, 1974). Visuo-spatial scratchpad was renamed as visuo-spatial sketch pad.

Revision note

With models like MSM and WMM an easy way to help learn them is to draw a blank outline of the 'boxes' for each model. Make several copies or keep an 'empty' copy saved as a file. You can fill in the blanks in different ways: with notes about duration, capacity or encoding (AO1) or with evidence for or against the existence of the store (AO2).

The episodic buffer

As well as dealing with incoming information, the CE needs to access LTM and transfer information back and forth between this and the slave units. It must be able to explain chunking, which uses meanings from LTM to link items and increase the capacity of STM. To do this, the CE would need to store as well as attend to and transfer information. This is the job of a third slave unit, the **episodic buffer**, which Baddeley (2000) added to the WMM. This has a limited storage capacity but allows the central executive to access LTM and exchange information between here and the other slave units.

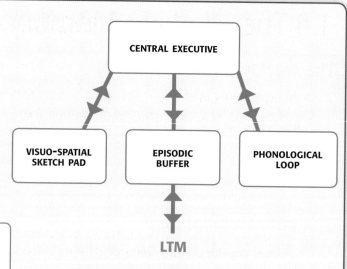

Figure 1.10 The working memory model: revised version (Baddeley, 2000).

Thinking psychologically

Salmon *et al.* (1996) used a PET scan (a scan of brain activity) to study activity levels in different parts of the brain. When the participants were doing visual or verbal tasks different areas were used. When the task also required the use of LTM to help with rehearsal, the areas were different again. Use the WMM to explain these findings.

Exam focus

Sally is playing Kaveman Kombat on her computer. She has to catapult rocks at sabre-toothed tigers and dodge clubs hurled by other cavemen. She happily plays while she is listening to her brother talking about why he likes a new sports shop, but when he explains how to get there, saying, 'Turn left out of school, then right along New Road', she keeps missing the tigers and getting hit by rocks. He gets excited as he watches the game and starts to talk really quickly then asks Sally what sabre-toothed tigers really used to eat and her game gets even worse.

According to the working memory model, there are different working memory functions. Use this model to explain Sally's successes and failures at the game. Refer to the scenario above in your answer.

(6 marks)

Alisha's answer:

Sally uses her iconic memory to deal with the visual information about the game and how the tigers and rocks are moving in space. She uses her echoic memory to listen to her brother talking about why he likes the sports shop. When he explains the directions this is spatial information too so she can't put it in the echoic memory with the positions of tigers and rocks so she gets hit. The central executive has to deal with all this information and when it comes quickly and she tries to recall from her LTM to remember what sabre-toothed tigers ate, there is too much at once so she gets killed. ⑤

Study note

One of the best ways to help yourself throughout your course is to use the information you have learned in real situations.

Over the next few minutes think of one task that has used your visuo-spatial sketch pad, one that has used your phonological loop, one that has used your episodic buffer and one that has used your central executive.

Examiner commentary

This is a very good answer in two ways: it is closely linked to the source and it successfully explains the different aspects of Sally's sensory information in relation to the potential effect on memory. Unfortunately, Alisha has mistakenly called the VSSP the iconic memory and the PL the echoic memory. This is a frequent error – so watch out! Alisha's answer would therefore be 'generally accurate' rather than 'accurate', but as her response is essentially correct in its arguments, it would score 5 rather than 6. This is a shame as the content is sufficiently detailed to have earned all 6 marks if the mislabelling had been avoided.

1.5 Evaluating the Working Memory Model

Strengths of the working memory model

➕ *Evidence* supports the PL, e.g. Baddeley *et al.* (1975) found that words that take a long time to say are not remembered as well as ones that are quick to say.

➕ *Evidence* also supports the VSSP, e.g. Seitz & Schumann-Hengsteler (2000) showed that doing sums (a visual task) was disrupted more by visual than auditory distraction.

➕ Imbo *et al.* (2007) tested people doing sums with big numbers (affecting the CE) and which required 'carrying' (using the PL to hold the number 'in your head'). Both factors mattered, showing that both the CE and the PL are used.

➕ *Evidence* from brain scanning has shown that specific brain areas are associated with working memory. Compared to memorising with an unrelated distraction or no distraction, memorising with a task-related distractio, led to the greatest impairment and produced different patterns of brain activation (Dolcos *et al.*, 2007).

➕ The model has clinical *relevance* as it has been applied to help overcome cravings. McClelland *et al.* (2006) showed that distraction with a visuo-spatial task disrupted participants' ability to imagine foods, as both used the VSSP, so reduced their craving.

➕ Investigations into working memory have *relevance* to education. Oakhill *et al.* (1988) showed that reading speed and comprehension are linked to working memory span. Children with smaller working memories find understanding text hard so might need special help to assist them to pay attention to and retain information.

Weaknesses of the working memory model

➖ Some *evidence* contradicts the PL. Martin-Loeches *et al.* (1997) showed that auditory interference from sounds and speech, which should both affect the PL, did not activate the same brain area.

➖ *Evidence* conflicts with the VSSP. Farah *et al.* (1988) studied a brain-damaged patient with good spatial but poor visual processing, implying there are two systems, not one.

➖ *Evidence* also contradicts the CE. Eslinger & Damasio (1985) described a patient with brain damage whose CE seemed to work well as he had a high IQ and good reasoning. He could not, however, make decisions, suggesting that the CE is not a single system.

Exam focus

The working memory model suggests that there are different kinds of short-term store for different kinds of information. These separate subunits are controlled by the 'central executive'.

(a) Outline **two** strengths of the working memory model.
(2 marks + 2 marks)

(b) Outline **two** weaknesses of the working memory model.
(2 marks + 2 marks)

Derek's answer:

(a) The WMM is good because it has lots of evidence like Baddeley, Imbo and Dolcos. These show that there are three separate components in WM. ①

(b) However, other evidence suggests this might be wrong, for example some people with brain damage can cope with information about 3D space but not visual information which you wouldn't expect if the VSSP was just one system that dealt with all visuo-spatial information because they should either be good at both or neither. ② Using fMRI scans, researchers have shown that brain activation happens in different places during different kinds of sound-based memory tasks like noise and words which you wouldn't expect if the PL was just one thing. ②

Examiner commentary

Derek's answer to part (a) makes a valid point, hinting at appropriate evidence, but has no accurate elaboration – he needed to report findings not just names. His answer to (b) is accurate and elaborated. The names are missing but he has used the findings of studies to demonstrate how the evidence contradicts the model. However, spell out what abbreviations mean the first time you write them, especially if it is one that you have made up.

1.6 Memory in Everyday Life: strategies for memory improvement

Using of cues

Cues are pieces of information that we encode at the same time as a to-be-remembered item and which can later help us with recall. A **context cue** is an external part of the learning situation, e.g. something we can see, hear or smell. **State cues** are internal, including the way we feel, such as being scared or sad. We therefore remember better if we are in the same place, or surrounded by similar things, and when we are in the same emotional or physiological condition as when we memorised the information. Categories can also act as cues. When Tulving & Pearlstone (1966) provided meaningful headings for groups of words, participants recalled more than if they did not have these cues. When the participants without the headings as cues were then given them, their recall improved.

Do context and state cues work?

Ideas about the importance of cues are supported by evidence such as Baker *et al.* (2004) who tested people's learning and recall whilst chewing or not chewing gum. Those in the same condition for both learning and retrieval (e.g. chewing gum in both conditions) performed better on immediate recall than those who were in a different condition (e.g. chewing gum in one condition and not chewing gum in the other) showing that the context of having or not having gum affected recall. Godden & Baddeley (1975) produced similar results for longer-term recall of words when the context was either the same or different with regard to whether the participants were on land or under water. Similarly, Mead & Ball (2007) found that the cue of music, either in a minor key (sounding sad) or a major key (sounding happy), affected feelings and produced a state-dependent effect as participants recalled better when they were in the same emotional state as they had been during encoding.

Cues and exams

As a strategy to improve recall, the context and state during retrieval need to resemble those experienced during learning. For exams, this means making sitting at your desk in the exam hall like being at home or in class. The context would be similar if you used a see-through pencil case all year then took it into your exams; though beware of having only one 'favourite pen' – if it breaks in the exam and you have to use another it might have exactly the opposite effect. To provide the same state cues, you need to stay relaxed in your exams. The best way to do this is to revise well – so keep reading!

Meaningful cues – like categories – help with retrieval so you can use this strategy in your revision and in exams too. When you are writing revision notes try to put a useful heading at the top of each page or section; write things like 'evidence for the phonological loop' rather than just 'WMM'. When you tackle a difficult question in an exam it is useful to write a few notes first; these keywords can act as cues to help you to recall later.

Cues and eyewitnesses

Context and state cues can also be used to help eyewitnesses. Think about how you would feel if you saw a building in flames, or a shooting. When a witness sees a crime they may experience specific state cues, for instance they may be very frightened. There may also be specific environmental cues, such as the presence of particular cars, the smell of burning or it might be dark. When recalling the event at home, in a police station or in court they will be more relaxed and many of the features of the physical situation might be different. Crime scene reconstruction helps to overcome this; by having people acting out probable events in the same place, context cues are provided. Additionally, emotions may be reinstated by the situation, providing state cues. These will maximise the possibility of witnesses remembering other things they may have seen or heard at the time.

Study note

You might want to check the ideas you had about tasks that might have used your working memory (see Study note on page 8). Here are some possibilities:

- visuo-spatial sketch pad: looking at Figure 1.10, imagining the Kaveman Kombat game or the layout of the roads described by Sally's brother
- phonological loop: talking to someone else about what you have read, listening to the radio, imagining the sound of chewing gum, imagining sad or happy music
- episodic buffer: recalling the meaning of words, e.g. what context and state cues are
- central executive: all of the above.

Using mnemonics

A *mnemonic* is a memory aid. Many mnemonic techniques use cues, which can be semantic or visual. Semantic cues involve organising the material to be learned so that it is meaningful and easy to retrieve. The *peg-word system* uses an existing sequence of numbers and rhyming words in memory. This structure provides semantic and visual cues so the new items are easier to recall. The *method of loci* uses a familiar route (a series of places, or 'locations') to help recall. The sequence of to-be-remembered items are visualised along a path, such as a habitual journey or the view around a well-known room.

The peg-word system

Lily needs to remember lots of things for school. She visualises them like this:

One–bun   Her red **rubber** looks like a cherry on the top of a bun.
Two–shoe   Her **flute** is stuffed inside a shoe.
Three–tree   Her painting **apron** is dangling from a tree.
Four–door   Her geography **book** is huge and standing in the doorway.
Five–hive   Her **watch** face looks like a flower with bees on in front of a hive.
Six–sticks   Her **pencils** are all in a heap on the floor mixed up with lots of sticks.
Seven–heaven   Her **pencil sharpener** is all shiny and peeping out from behind a cloud in heaven.
Eight–gate   Her **sandwich box** is balanced on top of a gate.
Nine–wine   Her **water bottle** is standing next to a wine glass.
Ten–hen   A hen is running away with her PE **shorts** in its beak.

This is a good system because both semantic and visual cues are used and the items can be recalled in a particular order.

Method of loci

Sean is on holiday and putting up his tent in the dark. He can't remember whether to assemble the frame made of poles, the inner net or the waterproof outer layer first. And he isn't sure when to put the guy ropes on or whether the doors should be zipped closed first. He has done it before, but has forgotten when to do each thing.

Using the method of loci, Sean could memorise the correct order by imagining each item in a specific place along a familiar route. To recall the items, the route is visualised and the new material can be easily accessed using the scene as a cue. For example, if Sean used the journey from the college library to the gates, he could picture zipping books together in the library, lots of poles across the library door, water flowing down the stairs from the library, twitching net curtains in the house opposite the entrance, then everyone swinging along the exit road on ropes like Tarzan. This sounds bizarre, but the sillier the mental image the more likely it is to be remembered, because it is distinctive. Using a familiar route structures the sequence so the cues are organised and the images of the to-be-remembered items can be recalled easily and in order.

Figure 1.11 The method of loci would be a good way of recalling the order of construction.

Exam focus

Claud knows his way out of the house, past the postbox and the cottage with big chimneys to the village shop with its window boxes of flowers and big yellow front door. But even though he only tries to remember five things he needs to buy, he always forgets some of them.

Using the information described above, outline a strategy Claud could use to improve his memory for the things he needs to buy.   *(3 marks)*

Yogita's answer:

Claud should use the method of loci as this has been shown to be effective. ①

Examiner commentary

Identifying a method only earns one mark; the question is asking for application, e.g. by explaining how the method is used and relating this to Claud, for example linking each item of shopping – which you can make up – to the house, postbox, chimneys, flowers, and so on.

1.7 Memory in Everyday Life: factors affecting eyewitness testimony

Eyewitness testimony

Eyewitnesses report evidence to the police to help with finding or convicting criminals. The reliability of their testimonies is therefore important. However, many factors can affect their accuracy, such as witness anxiety, their age and misleading information.

Anxiety and arousal in eyewitnesses

If witnesses are faced with a frightening crime scene, their field of view shrinks (Oue *et al.*, 2001) so they notice less and remember fewer important details. Loftus *et al.* (1987) showed that eyewitnesses were less likely to remember a criminal's face when they were carrying a weapon because it draws their attention. However, sometimes more risky crime scenes produce better recall. Hosch and Cooper (1982) found that participants were more likely to identify a 'thief' if they had stolen the participant's own watch than another person's calculator – because this was more stressful.

The Yerkes-Dodson Law says that performance is best in moderately arousing conditions, so recall would be worse in very high or very low arousal situations. Parker *et al.* (2006) found that memory for a hurricane was related to how badly an individual was affected. People who had suffered most and least had the poorest memory showing that a moderate amount of anxiety can improve memory in real situations, but that extremes worsen it.

Yuille & Cutshall (1986) investigated the recall of witnesses to a murder. Those who had higher levels of arousal recalled fewer correct facts than those with lower levels, supporting the Yerkes-Dodson Law. However, those with very high arousal levels were *better* than those with moderate levels. This might be because the witnesses closest to the crime scene would be most stressed but would also have the clearest view.

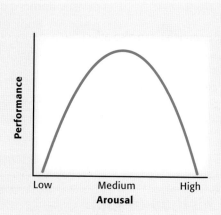

Figure 1.12 The Yerkes-Dodson 'inverted U' Law.

Anxiety and retrieval in eyewitnesses

According to Freud's idea of repression, eyewitnesses may be unable to retrieve traumatic memories of crime scenes. This suggests that we are motivated to forget unpleasant memories to protect ourselves from them. Köhler *et al.* (2002) found that the more stress-inducing words are, the worse they are remembered, supporting the idea of repression, but Hadley & MacKay (2006) found the opposite – more stressful words were remembered better! So, although repression might cause a reduction in eyewitness accuracy, frightening aspects of a crime scene might alternatively enhance recall.

Misleading information and eyewitnesses

When we encode and retrieve information it is not recorded perfectly like a photograph that can be looked at again and is exactly the same. The idea of **reconstruction** says instead that memories are 'rebuilt' from stored elements when they are retrieved. During this process, we can be misled by additional 'post-event' information. Loftus & Palmer (1974) showed that information provided by leading questions heard after seeing a car crash scene could change memory. Participants asked questions about the cars which 'smashed' into each other estimated that they were travelling faster than those asked about cars which 'hit' each other. They were also more likely to report having seen (non-existent) broken glass. When the memory is reconstructed, both the crash scene and the verb 'smashed' are incorporated into the memory, so greater speed estimates and the 'recall' of broken glass are likely.

Lindsay (1990) showed that even when participants are told that misleading information is incorrect it still affects their recall – but only when it is similar to reality.

Study note

Loftus has conducted many different studies on eyewitness testimony. It is important that, if you have learned about more than one, you don't get them muddled up. One way to avoid this is to use visual imagery. For example, to remember Loftus & Palmer you could imagine watching through a broken glass pane of a window as cars speed past a line of <u>palm</u> trees and crash.

Age and eyewitness testimony: child witnesses and misleading information

Children don't always understand what adults say, especially if they ask complex questions like lawyers do in court, so their testimonies may be unreliable. Carter *et al.* (1996) found that children found it harder to answer questions correctly if they were in 'legalese', e.g. 'To the best of your knowledge, X, in fact, kissed you, didn't she?' than 'X kissed you, didn't she?' Both use the tag 'didn't she' so are leading questions (page 12). Krackow & Lynn (2003) investigated the use of such questions which could be asked in child abuse cases, using a game of Twister. When the children were asked about whether they were touched, more answered the tagged question 'Amy touched your bottom, didn't she?' incorrectly than the direct question 'Did Amy touch your bottom?'

Lewis *et al.* (1995) showed children photographs of adult males in a line-up, one of which was (incorrectly) labelled 'Daddy'. When later asked 'Is this man your daddy?' 29 per cent of the children said yes to the man previously labelled as 'Daddy'. This shows that children are affected by leading information but that, even aged 3–4 years, the effect is quite small.

Age and eyewitness testimony: child witnesses and stereotypes

Stereotypes can also affect the accuracy of children's testimonies. In a study by Memon *et al.* (2006), children were told a story about 'Jim' by their teacher. The children met 'Jim' a few days later and were asked questions about the visit. If Jim was described positively in the story, this stereotype caused them to identify positive things about his visit that were false. However, if Jim was described negatively in the story, this did not affect their later memory of his visit. This suggests that people with stereotypically positive features are less likely to be considered guilty by children.

Age and eyewitness testimony: elderly eyewitnesses

Wright & Holliday (2005) found that police officers believed adults aged over 60 years to be less reliable and thorough as witnesses than younger people. Brimacombe *et al.* (1997) compared recall of a crime seen on video by elderly and younger adults, and found the older adults were less accurate. Their testimonies, when viewed by other participants and when transcribed (without information about their ages), were rated as less credible. These differences could not have arisen from negative stereotypes about older adults so it is important to try to improve the reliability of the testimonies of older adults.

In a comparison of young (17–31 years), young-old (60–74 years) and old-old (75–95 years) witnesses, Wright & Holliday (2007) also found recall became less complete and accurate with age. However, when they used **cognitive interviews** (page 14) rather than standard ones, both groups of older adults recalled more details accurately.

Exam focus

A little boy called Tim and his granddad, Harold, witnessed a robbery. They saw the criminal run out of a shop and get away in a car so might be able to remember lots of useful details.

Age is an important factor in eyewitness testimony. For **one** of the people in the source, explain how their age may affect the accuracy of their testimony.

(3 marks)

Bill's answer:

Krackow & Lynn showed children's accuracy is worse if they are asked misleading questions. ✗ Tim's granddad is unlikely to be a good witness unless he gets a cognitive interview because memory declines with age, though according to Wright & Holliday if his granddad was <u>really</u> old he'd be worse than if he was only 60. ③

Examiner commentary

Bill has tried to explain two people – only the better one would earn marks as the question only asks for one person. The 'child' section doesn't make direct reference to Tim (although it is implicit as it refers to 'children') and is weaker. The second section refers to the source explicitly and is an elaborated answer.

1.8 Memory in Everyday Life: the cognitive interview

Cognitive interviewing and misleading information

Misleading information, including the way witnesses are questioned, affects the accuracy of testimonies. Loftus & Palmer (1974) showed how single words affected speed estimates and reporting of broken glass, and Lewis *et al.* (1995) showed that children's identification of people in a line-up could be misled using labels. Krackow & Lynn (2003) reported that direct questions produced more accurate answers from children than ones with misleading tags. The cognitive interview makes use of such ideas to improve eyewitness accuracy.

The principles of the cognitive interview

Geiselman *et al.* (1985) identified four key principles for the cognitive interview:

1. *Recreate internal and environmental cues* – cues present at the time of the crime will be encoded with information that may be useful in the testimony so can help the witness to access those memories. They can be internal (state) cues, e.g. emotions, or environmental (context) cues, i.e. things they could see, hear or smell (see cue-dependent memory, page 10).
2. *Report everything* – even details about the incident that are incomplete or apparently irrelevant can act as triggers to cue the retrieval of other, useful, memories. This makes sense as long-term memory uses semantic encoding (page 4) so one memory can lead to another.
3. *Report information in different orders* – details about the incident should not just be given chronologically (starting with what happened first in time) but from different starting points, e.g. earlier in the day or from the first shout they heard.
4. *Report the incident from different perspectives* – the witness is asked to consider what someone else might have heard or seen, for example if they had been standing behind the criminal or were upstairs.

Geiselman *et al.* (1985) (like Wright & Holliday, page 13), found that cognitive interviewing improved the recall of detail by witnesses without loss of accuracy.

The enhanced cognitive interview

Fisher *et al.* (1987) have expanded the ideas to develop the enhanced cognitive interview (ECI), which has four further principles:

1. *Distractions should be minimised* – this includes the minimising of intrusion by police questioning (e.g. letting the witness pause or go 'er' and 'um' a lot). Long-term memories are recalled through short-term memory in which interference causes displacement (see page 3) so this should improve accuracy.
2. *Slow the witness's reporting speed* – if witnesses are rushed this can act as a source of interference.
3. *Pause between questions* – gaps should allow individual witnesses enough time between one idea and the next.
4. *Reduce witness anxiety* – this should be reduced as stress can interfere with recall.

They found this technique was more effective than basic cognitive interviewing. Many more correct statements were recalled but there were also more 'false positives' (i.e. extra 'recalled' information about things that didn't happen). In a real-world setting, Fisher *et al.* (1989) found that 46 per cent more statements were obtained from witnesses using ECI and that these were over 90 per cent accurate when checked against a second witness.

Exam focus

Indicate whether each statement below is true or false by ticking **one** box only on each line.   *(3 marks)*

	True	False
1. A cognitive interview helps recall by using internal cues.		
2. In cognitive interviewing witnesses only report what's directly relevant.		
3. Cognitive interviewers can ask what someone else might have seen.		

Examiner commentary
Read true/false questions carefully – the second line looks true, but isn't.
(Answers: 1 True, 2 False, 3 True.)

1.9 Summary

MULTI-STORE MODEL

The **multi-store model** (Atkinson and Shiffrin, 1968) is a theory from **cognitive psychology**. It proposes three stores that **encode** information differently and have different **capacities** and **durations**.

Short-term sensory store

The **short-term sensory store** (STSS) holds information from the senses in a **modality specific** code for a very short time. The **iconic store** holds visual items and the **echoic store** holds sound-based items.

Short-term memory

Short-term memory (STM) has a slightly longer duration (less than 30 seconds) and a limited capacity of 7±2 chunks. The information is encoded acoustically.

Long-term memory

Long-term memory (LTM) lasts minutes to years and encodes semantically (by meaning). It also has a very large capacity.

Control processes

Rehearsal is a control process in the model. It maintains information in STM and moves it from STM to LTM.

STM/LTM differences

Evidence from **serial position tasks**, differences between errors on **immediate** and **delayed recall** and case studies of people with **amnesia** show that STM and LTM are different stores.

Interference

Interference causes forgetting from STM because items are displaced.

Multiple STM stores

Other evidence suggests that STM is not a simple acoustic store – it can encode semantically too, and because visual and acoustic information interfere, STM may hold visual items too.

Multiple LTM stores

LTM is not a single store because different types of LTMs can be affected independently, e.g. in amnesics.

WORKING MEMORY MODEL

The **working memory model** is an explanation for short-term memory, which can explain how different types of encoding seem to be used in STM.

Phonological loop

The **phonological loop** (PL) stores acoustically coded items for 2–3 seconds (longer with rehearsal) but this is affected by the time it takes to non-verbally 'repeat' any item. Verbal interference prevents rehearsal and reduces recall.

Central executive

Baddeley & Hitch (1974) proposed the **central executive** (CE) (an organising unit that sorts and redirects information from the senses), the phonological loop (which holds sound-based information) and the visuo-spatial sketch pad (which holds visual and spatial information).

Central executive

The **central executive** uses information encoded in any form as it takes information from the senses or from LTM and sends it to the phonological loop or visuo-spatial sketch pad. It selectively attends to information and divides attention between tasks.

Visuo-spatial sketch pad

The **visuo-spatial sketch pad** (VSSP) can process verbal information when the phonological loop is busy, but is less effective if interference is visual.

Episodic buffer

The **episodic buffer** was added to the model by Baddeley (2000). This unit gives the central executive access to information in LTM, which it can hold temporarily.

Strengths of WMM

Evidence shows that using the same slave unit for two simultaneous tasks makes them slower or more difficult. This may explain why the size of working memory matters to educational success. It can also reduce food craving by stopping visual imagery.

Weaknesses of WMM

Noise and speech do not affect the same brain area, and a brain-damaged patient had problems with visual but not spatial processes. This suggests that neither the PL nor the VSSP are single systems. Another patient had a high IQ but poor reasoning so the CE may not be a single system either.

IMPROVING MEMORY BY USING CUES

Cues are encoded when we store to-be-remembered items. **Context cues** are external, e.g. parked cars or barking dogs. **State cues** are internal, e.g. emotions. We recall better with the same cues at encoding and recall. **Categories** can also act as cues – they are semantic ones.

Context cues from encoding and retrieving in the same place (e.g. on land or in water) help recall, as does having matching state cues from sad or happy sounding music during encoding and recall. Category headings help recall even if present only at recall because they are meaningful.

Using cues

In exams, having things on your desk that you had at home or in class can act as a context cue. Staying calm in exams provides the same state cues as when you learned the information. Semantic cues help LTM so revision notes should have meaningful headings and jotting down keywords in exams can act as a cue to help with difficult questions.

Crime scene reconstruction provides context cues to eyewitnesses. If the scene evokes emotions, state cues can also help them to retrieve other memories encoded at the time.

IMPROVING MEMORY BY USING MNEMONICS

Mnemonics are memory aids. The **peg-word system** uses a sequence of numbers and words to structure encoding. Items are encoded linked to visual images from the 'One–bun, two–shoe' rhyme. When the rhyme is repeated this cues the recall of the new items. In the **method of loci**, new items are encoded in locations along a familiar route. When the route is visualised later, the new items can be recalled in their positions along the sequence.

Using mnemonics

Peg-word and method of loci associations are most easily retrieved if they are distinctive. Like the peg-word rhyme, the method of loci route should be very familiar so that the cues are readily retrieved. Both strategies help to recall items in order, but only for lists of concrete things (e.g. things that we could see or feel).

ANXIETY AND AROUSAL IN EYEWITNESSES

Frightened witnesses notice and recall less especially if the criminal has a weapon. Some evidence shows that they recall better if the crime affects them directly – which ought to be more stressful – so according to repression they should recall very little.

Yerkes-Dodson Law

The Yerkes-Dodson Law says that our recall is better with moderate arousal but worse if arousal is very high or low. This applies to real-world recall such as of a hurricane disaster. Sometimes witnesses closest to a crime – with very high arousal – recall better than less stressed ones, possibly because they have the best view.

MISLEADING INFORMATION AND EYEWITNESSES

Memory is **reconstructive**; it is 'rebuilt' during retrieval so can be affected by information received after encoding. Leading questions provide additional information and distort recall, e.g. making people think cars were travelling fast because they were described as having 'smashed' into each other.

Child witnesses

Children's testimonies are unreliable if they are asked misleading questions, e.g. ending in 'didn't they?' If children hold, or are misled by, stereotypes this can also reduce the accuracy of their testimonies – but evidence suggests that this is only if the stereotypes are positive.

Elderly eyewitnesses

The police believe that older adults are poor witnesses and evidence supports this, but if elderly witnesses are given cognitive interviews, their accuracy improves.

THE COGNITIVE INTERVIEW

The four key principles for **cognitive interviewing** are: **recreating internal and environmental cues**, and getting witnesses to report: **incomplete or irrelevant details**, information in **different orders** and the incident from **different viewpoints**. This technique improves the detail recalled without loss of accuracy.

1.10 Cognitive Psychology Scenarios

Scenario 1: Dario and the dragons

Multi-store model

Dario has played games like Dungeons and Dragons for years. He can remember lots of information like battle strategies, places, names and numbers. Dario hates being disturbed, though. His mum will shout for him and he instantly forgets what he was doing. On any one day, he finds that the faster the game goes, the harder it is to remember what happened at the beginning of a session. He's okay if he needs to recall where a dragon was just a moment ago, but he soon forgets. Sometimes at school he drifts off into his fantasy land in the middle of a lesson and finally hears, 'DARIO! What did I just say?', and somewhere, in the depths of his mind, he can hear exactly what the teacher has asked.

Use your understanding of the multi-store model to explain as many aspects of Dario's memory as you can.

Strategies for memory improvement

A new version of Dario's favourite game has just come out and he wants to be one of the highest scorers. He talks to his older brother, who is studying psychology at college.

Use your understanding of ways to improve memory to identify what Dario's brother might suggest to help him to remember all the new names, routes and monsters in the latest game.

Working memory model

When the game strategy uses Dario's navigational skill at the same time as his ability to listen out for threats, he manages really well. But when he has to find his way by plotting his route in his head and look around the screen for danger he finds the game much more difficult. If a game gets really frantic, with lots of things going on at the same time, Dario feels like his head is going into overload and he starts to get muddled over the simplest things.

Use your understanding of the working memory model to explain as many aspects of Dario's memory as you can.

Revision note

When you are answering open-ended questions try to use several different ideas in your answer. Remember to look at the number of marks being awarded for the question — that will guide the amount of detail you need to give.

Scenario 2: Exams and eyewitnesses

Eyewitness testimony

Kirsten is on her way to her afternoon Psychology exam and is walking with her grandma who is taking her little brother back to nursery school. Kirsten has her mascot in her bag which she has had on her desk whenever she's been revising. As she comes around the corner by the petrol station she sees a boy and a girl wearing crash helmets leap on motorcycles and race away. Each one has a rucksack on their back. The manager of the petrol station comes running out behind them and demands to know if Kirsten got a good look at the two lads that have stolen the morning's takings.

Use your understanding of the effect of misleading information to explain what might happen to Kirsten's memory of the events she has witnessed.

Explain whether witness accounts from **either** Kirsten's grandma **or** her little brother might differ in their accuracy from Kirsten's.

Strategies for improving memory

When Kirsten gets to her exam, she feels really confident. She has revised hard and has her mascot on her desk. The invigilator picks it up and says it will distract other candidates because it is a bright orange troll and tells her she can collect it at the end of the exam. Kirsten is still upset from the scene at the petrol station and this makes her even more nervous. She opens her paper and reaches for a pen out of the pencil case she always uses in class. When Kirsten walks out of the exam she is met by a police officer who wants to take a statement about the events she witnessed at the petrol station.

Use your understanding of the effect of anxiety on memory to explain **either** why Kirsten may not recall very well in the exam **or** why she may not recall very well when she gives her statement to the police officer.

Kirsten believes she has revised hard. Describe **one** strategy that Kirsten may have used to help her to remember things for the exam.

Cognitive interviewing

The police officer says they are trying out a new procedure to help witnesses.

Why might the police choose to use a cognitive interview to help Kirsten to accurately recall the events she saw?

Study note

Psychology is about people and everyday life. Try to get into the habit of using what you know about psychology and talking about it. Maybe you can explain why your brother keeps forgetting his football boots or help your grand-dad to remember which of his four grand-children dislike apples, bananas, oranges and peaches. Each time you forget something, try to explain why it might have happened in two different ways. Which one is more likely?

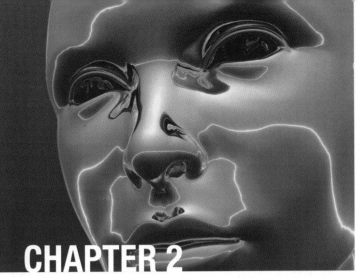

CHAPTER 2
Developmental Psychology

2.1 An Introduction to Developmental Psychology

YOU NEED TO:

know what these terms mean:

- developmental psychology
- attachment
- privation
- institutionalisation

describe and evaluate:

- the learning theory of attachment
- the evolutionary theory of attachment
- Bowlby's theory of attachment
- Ainsworth's research

be able to explain:

- types of attachment
- cultural variations in attachment
- how attachments fail

understand and apply your knowledge about attachment, including:

- the impact of day care on children's social development
- what research has told us about attachment and day care practices

KEY TERMS

developmental psychology focuses on how the human mind and behaviour change over the lifespan. As childhood is a time of rapid change, this is a key aspect

attachment a close two-way emotional relationship between two people such as a child and a parent. An attached infant stays close to its carer (*proximity seeking*) and uses them as a secure base from which to explore. When separated they get anxious (*separation distress*) and distrust unfamiliar adults (*stranger anxiety*)

privation the failure of an infant to form an attachment, e.g. when they are severely neglected or abused

institutionalisation the consequences for a child's attachment and behaviour when they spend much of their time being cared for away from the home, such as in an orphanage

2.2 Early Explanations of Attachment

Attachment

Within **developmental psychology** many phases of life are investigated. Here we focus on early changes and the strong bond, or **attachment**, between an infant and its carer.

Learning theory and attachment

We can learn by associating events (**classical conditioning**) or by repeating actions that are rewarded (**operant conditioning**). Infants are fed very often – and love it. As food is usually given by the same person, they associate the pleasure of eating with that individual so learn to love them too. This is a classical conditioning explanation:

Initially:

Unconditioned stimulus (UCS) **food**	→	Unconditioned response (UCR) **love**
Neutral stimulus (NS) **carer**	→	No response

The infant is then fed many times by the same person:

UCS (**food**) + NS (**carer**)	→	Unconditioned response (UCR) **love**

After the infant has been fed many times by the same person:

Conditioned stimulus (CS) **carer**	→	Conditioned response (CR) **love**

Figure 2.1 Classical conditioning of attachment.

Harlow (1958)

Harlow observed the behaviour of baby monkeys with surrogate mechanical mothers. These were either hard or cuddly and some did, whilst others did not, provide milk. The monkeys preferred the soft towelling (cuddly) mothers even if they did not produce food. Baby monkeys with only a wire mother were more stressed generally and monkeys with soft mothers explored more, running back to them when shown a scary drumming bear toy. These findings suggest that attachment is governed by comfort rather than food.

Figure 2.2 Harlow's monkeys became attached to the cuddly mothers even if they didn't offer food.

Adults are operantly conditioned to love babies. Feeding them when they cry stops the crying or makes them smile, rewarding (or 'reinforcing') the loving behaviour of the adult. Smiling is a positive reinforcer – it is nice when it happens. When the baby's crying ceases this is a negative reinforcer – it is nice when it stops. Both positive and negative reinforcers *increase* the frequency of the caring behaviour they follow. Importantly, babies are also operantly conditioned to love their carer. The baby's food is a positive reinforcer and the removal of discomfort – like being cold and wet – is a negative reinforcer.

Such simplistic explanations are, however, insufficient to account for the intense emotional nature of attachment. Also, attachments can form with people an infant meets often, even if they don't supply food.

Evolutionary theory and attachment

Evolution says that behaviours which aid survival and, importantly, reproduction, will be 'selected for', i.e. passed on if they are even only partly genetically controlled. Babies should therefore have evolved strategies that help them to survive and reach adulthood when they will reproduce successfully. We should therefore also find evidence that attachments in animals help their survival and reproduction.

Lorenz (1935) demonstrated **imprinting**: newly-hatched chicks (and some other species) form an attachment to the first moving object they see and follow it. This would normally be their mother so would help to keep them safe and fed. This occurs in a **critical period** early in life and affects their preferences as adults, e.g. to find the correct species for courtship and mating.

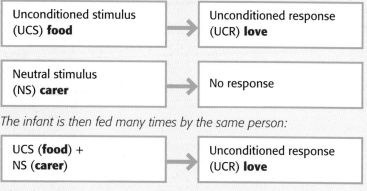

Well, you look like mummy...

Figure 2.3 Imprinting affects adult mate choice: being reared in a reptile house led to a peacock displaying to a giant tortoise.

Figure 2.4 Ducklings imprint on the mother duck.

2.3 Evaluating Early Explanations of Attachment

Strengths of learning theory

➕ *Evidence* from studies of classical and operant conditioning show that these processes do happen in people, so conditioning *could* play a role in attachment.

➕ Food certainly is reinforcing and babies are fed frequently, providing the requirements for learning to occur.

➕ *Evidence* suggests that emotional responses can be acquired through conditioning, e.g. learning to fear a situation through classical conditioning.

Strengths of evolutionary theory

➕ *Evidence*, such as Lorenz's, shows that imprinting matters for both survival and reproduction in animals, so simple attachments are affected by evolutionary processes. It is therefore likely that evolution has also influenced human attachment formation, for example explaining why adults like 'cute' baby-like faces with big eyes.

➕ Lorenz's idea of critical periods matters in humans too. If we don't form attachments early our later development is affected (page 20).

➕ The idea of a critical period has *relevance*, e.g. the importance of giving mothers with babies that need to be in incubators the opportunity to form an attachment.

> **Study note**
>
> You need to be able to apply ideas from animal research to humans. Lorenz's ducklings stayed by their mother who helped to protect them, led them away from danger and showed them what to eat. Harlow's monkeys showed secure base behaviour and proximity seeking to the cuddly mother. Such behaviours helped the survival of wild animals, and of early humans, by keeping them safe, but allowing them to explore and learn.

Weaknesses of learning theory

➖ The *evidence* supporting learning theory only successfully accounts for simple behaviours. Attachment is a complex and highly emotional response so is unlikely to be acquired through classical or operant conditioning alone.

➖ Babies form attachments to people they meet often, not just to those who feed them. Without food, conditioning explanations cannot readily explain how this can happen.

➖ *Evidence* from studies like Harlow's show that food alone is not enough for an attachment to form. Emotional comfort is more important.

➖ Bowlby's *alternative* theory (page 22) can account for findings such as Harlow's (page 20).

Weakness of evolutionary theory

➖ Evolution has clearly affected human attachments but they are more complex than imprinting.

Exam focus

Pair up each statement on the left with **one** term on the right.   *(3 marks)*

1. By giving male animals an image of the female of their species, attachment to the mother helps them to find a mate later.	a) Evolution
2. Breastfed babies repeatedly associate the mother with food.	b) Operant conditioning
3. Babies get hungry often. Being fed gets rid of the unpleasant feeling of hunger so they like the person who feeds them.	c) Classical conditioning

Examiner commentary

There is an important distinction between classical and operant conditioning. In classical conditioning something neutral (the carer) and something else (e.g. food) must appear *at the same time* to become associated. The response (in this case liking) transfers from one object to the other. Reinforcement in operant conditioning (negative in this example) occurs when a pleasant consequence *follows* a response. (Answers: 1a, 2c, 3b.)

2.4 Bowlby's Theory of Attachment

Bowlby's theory

Bowlby suggested that the role of the mother (or main carer) is unique and that their relationship with the child will affect future relationships. He called this special focus of attachment towards one person **monotropy**. This **instinctive** (natural) bond must form during a critical period early in the child's life. He believed that this relationship could have evolved because it is seen in a range of species and, early in human evolutionary history, would have helped to keep children safe from predators like wolves by staying near an adult for protection, signalling distress when left alone and returning to safety after exploring.

Evolution has selected behaviours in babies which elicit care from adults; these are called **social releasers** – like smiling and cooing. For the first two years babies are in a **sensitive period** during which they try to interact with adults and elicit care. If they fail it is much harder for them to form an attachment later. Brazelton *et al.* (1975) showed that social releasers, and parents' responses to them, are important to attachments. Mother and baby pairs imitated each other's movements (i.e. showed **interactional synchrony**) but if the mothers ignored the babies' social releasers the babies became distressed.

Figure 2.5 According to Bowlby babies instinctively elicit care from adults.

Internal working models

Bowlby (1969) developed Freud's idea that a child's first relationship serves as a prototype for later relationships, called an **internal working model**. This mental representation of how relationships work affects the child's own parenting behaviour later in life, reflecting the care – neglectful or positive – that they received. Bailey *et al.* (2007) found that teenage mothers who had insecure attachments to their own parents were likely to have insecurely attached children.

Exam focus

(a) Describe and evaluate **one** research study supporting Bowlby's theory.
(4 marks)

(b) Explain how the study you have described in part (a) relates to Bowlby's theory. *(4 marks)*

Examiner commentary

Karen's answer is quite basic. For part (a) she has chosen a suitable piece of evidence but the description doesn't say enough about the set-up (that there were various types of mother: food/no food, towelling/wire) and the description of the test of exploratory behaviour sounds as if she believes the monkeys were taken outside to see live bears (an 'open field' is simply a laboratory space with nothing in it other than the test objects – in this case a toy bear). She also could have described the conclusion – about the role of comfort in counteracting stress – and could have gone on to say how this affected their later behaviour – the maternally deprived monkeys had problems with mating and looking after their own offspring. However, Karen has attempted both the 'describe' and 'evaluate' aspects of the question and her evaluation point about generalising from animals, although too brief, is appropriate. Karen has not separated her answer into parts (a) and (b) and doesn't say how the study relates to Bowlby's theory, i.e. that it was supporting evidence because it shows that attachment formation is instinctive and how secure base behaviour links to the comfort an infant receives from their carer. She could have contrasted this with the idea that monkeys are, however, quite similar to us, more so than birds, so it is perhaps better evidence than Lorenz's, or that following up the monkeys into adulthood helped to show that early attachments matter throughout life.

Karen's answer:

Harlow tested monkeys which had grown up with surrogate mothers. They were put in a bear field that frightened them and they ran back to the fluffy mummy. People might behave differently than monkeys though. ③

2.5 Evaluating Bowlby's Theory of Attachment

Strengths of Bowlby's theory of attachment

➕ Bowlby's theory explains both *how* attachments form (e.g. the way carers respond to social releasers) and *why* (in terms of evolution).

➕ *Evidence* such as Brazelton *et al.*'s observational study shows that social processes (such as interactional synchrony) really are important in attachment formation and evidence from animal studies of imprinting, and monkeys' preferences for comforting mothers suggest that some aspects of attachment formation are innate.

➕ The similarity of the frequency of types of attachment across many cultures, such as secure attachments being most common, suggests that these are driven by inherited factors, i.e. are innate (e.g. *evidence* from van IJzendoorn & Kroonenberg, page 26).

➕ Monotropy suggests that the most sensitive carer will be the focus of an infant's attachment and is supported by *evidence* from the experimental findings of Brazelton *et al.* as the babies were distressed by an absence of response from the carer.

➕ Bailey *et al.*'s *evidence* showed that internal working models mattered as young mothers with insecure attachments themselves had insecurely attached babies.

➕ Bowlby's theory has real-life *relevance* for guiding the rehabilitation of individuals who have been abused as children so may have difficulty with parenting successfully.

Weaknesses of Bowlby's theory of attachment

➖ Evolutionary ideas are hard to test as we cannot look backwards in time and animals are not necessarily good models of early human development as they are too simplistic, and selection pressures operating on animals may have been different.

➖ Children will form attachments to several adults so monotropy – if seen as an exclusive bond to the mother – is too simplistic. An infant's attachment to their father as well as their mother can be important in development.

➖ Differences in attachments between individuals may *alternatively* be explained by temperament (personality). The innate behaviours of some infants may make them hard to respond to sensitively so their 'difficult' nature is worsened by poor attachment. This means it is hard to separate the factors responsible for insecurity.

➖ *Evidence* such as Fuertes *et al.* illustrates how infant temperament affects attachments (see page 25).

➖ Although there are cross-cultural similarities, there are also some differences and this suggests that at least some aspects of attachments are not innate (e.g. *evidence* from van IJzendoorn & Kroonenberg, page 26).

Exam focus

Billy's parents died when he was very young. He grew up in a small village with lots of his relations. His grandma fed him, changed his nappy and put him to bed according to a strict schedule, but his aunts and uncles also took turns to care for him. His aunt Stella spent time most days with him playing peek-a-boo and cuddling him – she loved his cute face and would tickle him each time he smiled.

(a) Explain how **either** learning theory **or** Bowlby's theory could account for Billy's attachment to one of his relations. *(4 marks)*

(b) Using a **different** theory from the one you used in part (a), explain why Billy might be attached to any other relation. *(3 marks)*

Gerrad's answer:

(a) Billy attached to Stella because Bowlby says she provided security and comfort. She also responded to his signals, like smiling. And he saw her often. ②

(b) Billy attached to his gran because of the positive reinforcement from her feeding him. ①

Examiner commentary

Both parts are correct and Gerrad has referred to the source, which is important in this question, but he needed to elaborate on his answers. Each point could be explained more fully and there are keywords relating to the theories such as 'operant conditioning' and 'sensitive responsiveness' that are missing.

2.6 Attachment Types

Attachment

Ainsworth (1967) identified three attachment types and Ainsworth & Wittig (1969) developed the 'Strange Situation' procedure to classify them. This technique measures the security of attachment a child displays towards its primary carer. The infant is observed in an unfamiliar setting, interacting with both familiar and unfamiliar people. There are seven key episodes, each lasting three minutes. In stage 1, the child and carer are placed in an empty room. In stage 2, the first used to measure responses, the child is encouraged to explore. After that, each new stage begins with one or both adults arriving or leaving the room (see Table 2.1).

Table 2.1 The Strange Situation.

Stage	Designed to measure	Carer present	Stranger present
1		✔	
2	Proximity seeking and secure base behaviour	✔	
3	Stranger anxiety	✔	✔
4	Stranger anxiety and separation distress		✔
5	Reuniting response	✔	
6	Separation distress		
7	Stranger anxiety		✔
8	Reuniting response	✔	

Attachment types

Based on the Strange Situation, Ainsworth proposed three attachment types: A, B and C (see Table 2.2). Type B is secure and Types A and C are insecure attachments.

Table 2.2 Attachment types.

Attachment type		Attachment behaviours					% British 12–18 month-olds
Letter	Name	Proximity seeking	Secure base	Separation distress	Reuniting response	Stranger anxiety	
A	Avoidant	✘	✘	✘	✘		20–25
B	Secure		✔	Moderate	✔	Moderate	60–75
C	Resistant	✔ (intense)		✔ (extreme)	✘		3

Some children show a mixture of Type A and Type C behaviours. Main & Solomon (1986) called this Type D attachment. These children may alternate between avoidant and resistant behaviour or combine them, e.g. staying close (proximity seeking) but resisting when reunited. They may freeze and appear to fear the primary carer or prefer the company of the unfamiliar person in the Strange Situation.

Exam focus

Indicate whether each statement below is true or false by ticking **one** box only on each line.

(3 marks)

	True	False
1. Securely attached infants are very distressed by separation from their carer.	☐	☐
2. Infants with resistant attachments stay close to their carer.	☐	☐
3. An absence of the reuniting response is characteristic of infants with avoidant attachments.	☐	☐

Examiner commentary
Remember, it is not impossible for all the answers to be true or all to be false. You need to consider each statement on its own. (Answers: 1 False, 2 True, 3 True.)

2.7 Investigating Attachment: Ainsworth's research

Maternal sensitivity hypothesis

Ainsworth suggested that attachment type depends on the behaviour of the main carer towards the child, especially that sensitive responsiveness matters in developing a secure attachment. This is the ability of the adult carer to notice and respond appropriately to signals from the baby. Type A and C attachments are the result of insensitive parenting, where the carer doesn't respond to the baby's cues. Type A children cope with anxiety by emotionally distancing themselves from adults so they are not disappointed by a lack of response from their carer. Type Cs maintain close proximity and become angry when left alone and when reunited. This enables the infant to 'control' the carer.

Stayton & Ainsworth (1973) demonstrated the link between sensitive responsiveness and attachment types in a study of infants and their mothers at home. They found that mothers with lower levels of sensitive responsiveness had babies who spent more time crying. Cantero & Cerezo (2001) also observed mother–infant interactions. They too found that Type B attachment was associated with maternal sensitivity whilst Type A attachment was linked to controlling or rejecting parenting and Type C to a lack of parental responsiveness.

Other factors affecting the security of attachment

Ainsworth's ideas about maternal sensitivity are clearly important but other factors may also affect the success of attachments. Donovan *et al.* (2007) found that 'insensitive' mothers – with low sensitive responsiveness – had problems processing information from their babies' signals. Mothers of six-month-old babies who found it hard to judge emotion from pictures of babies' faces had lower levels of sensitive responsiveness and were more likely to have insecurely attached babies at two years.

Scher & Mayseless (2000) investigated lifestyle factors and found that children were more likely to be Type C if they spent longer each day in nursery care and if their mothers were stressed or worked long hours.

The child's temperament (its personality) is also important. Fuertes *et al.* (2006) found that the temperament of some infants makes them difficult to respond to so secure attachments are harder to forge.

Attachment and adulthood

Ainsworth (1989) suggested that attachment type remained fairly stable over a child's life and that it would lead to particular patterns of behaviour in adulthood. Being securely attached is an advantage for adults when parenting their own children and in their success with friendships and romantic relationships. McCarthy (1999) supports Ainsworth's ideas in relation to later relationships. Forty women aged 25 to 44 who had been assessed for attachment type as children were followed up. They were tested for current attachment type and asked about their adult friendships and romantic relationships. They found that:

- Type Bs had good friendships and romantic relationships
- Type Cs had problems with friendships
- Type As had problems with romantic relationships
- Type Ds had problems with all relationships.

Banse (2004) investigated the link between attachment type and marital satisfaction. When both partners were Type Bs they had the highest levels of satisfaction. Insecure attachment types correlated negatively with satisfaction.

Figure 2.6 Secure attachments are important to effective adult relationships

2.8 Cultural Variations in Attachment

Van IJzendoorn & Kroonenberg

Van IJzendoorn & Kroonenberg (1988) investigated cultural variations in attachment type. By combining the findings of 32 studies of attachment type which used the Strange Situation they compared the frequency of attachment types in eight different countries – *inter*cultural comparisons. They also looked at more than one sample within some cultures (i.e. *intra*cultural comparisons).

In all countries secure attachment (Type B) was the most common and in most (except China, Japan and Israel) anxious resistant (Type C) was the least common. Germany had the highest frequency of insecure-avoidant, whilst Japan and Israel had very few. This suggests that whilst the Strange Situation finds some differences between cultures these are small. The variation within cultures was nearly 1.5 times greater than that between cultures. For example in one Israeli sample the percentages for Types A, B and C were 9, 57 and 34 respectively, whilst for another they were 3, 81 and 16. Likewise in the US, one sample gave percentages of 5, 94 and 1 whilst another produced an entirely different pattern of 21, 46 and 33 per cent. The US average, however, of 21, 65 and 14 per cent does seem to be typical in that Type B is universally the most common attachment type. Differences between cultures or subcultures might be due to different child-rearing practices or may reflect the usefulness or otherwise of the Strange Situation as a measure of attachment across cultures.

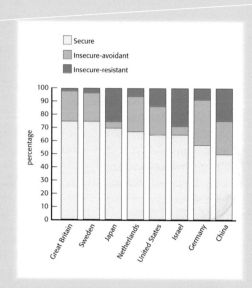

Figure 2.7 Attachment types in different cultures.

Explaining cultural variations: cultural, artificial and evolutionary differences

Grossman & Grossman (1990) suggest that a 'good' attachment might mean different things to different cultures. In Britain and America, an emotionally distant child is seen as a problem, so Type A avoidant attachment is perceived negatively. In contrast, German culture values independence so more Type As would be expected in Germany than in Britain. This explanation assumes that real differences do exist between cultures.

Alternatively, apparent cultural variations might be the product of Strange Situation. It was developed in the US and may not work effectively in all cultures. Takahashi (1990) suggests that it is ineffective in Japan because mothers and babies are rarely separated. This cultural norm would tend to produce high levels of separation anxiety. Measures of the reuniting response may also be distorted because Japanese mothers tend to rush to the child and pick it up so the infant's reaction is difficult to measure. The combination of being unable to observe a reuniting response and high separation anxiety means that many Japanese children may have been incorrectly classified as Type C. This would suggest that the Strange Situation, and attachment theory in general, are culture bound, i.e. apply only to the cultures in which they were developed, i.e. to Europe and America.

Belsky (1999) suggested that differences between cultures may exist but that rather than being culturally driven they are evolutionary in origin. Different attachment types are useful for people living in different environments. In harsh environments where mortality is high it is beneficial to form shallow adult relationships and have sex early – this maintains the population and reduces the sense of loss when partners die young. Insecure attachments are linked to early sexual activity and superficial adult relationships – they should therefore be more common. Furthermore, as a high-mortality environment is stressful, levels of maternal sensitivity will be lower, again increasing the rate of insecure attachment.

Figure 2.8 Are cross-cultural differences in attachment real?

2.9 Privation

Disruption to the formation and maintenance of attachments

Rutter (1981) distinguished between deprivation (a temporary or permanent separation from the attachment figure) and **privation** (the failure to form an attachment). Deprivation (or separation) can be short-term, e.g. day care, or long-term, e.g. due to hospitalisation of mother or child, family breakdown or the death of a parent. Privation can result from severe neglect, abuse or growing up in an institution without the chance to form attachments.

The maternal deprivation hypothesis

Bowlby *et al.* (1952) proposed the maternal deprivation hypothesis, suggesting that separation during a child's first two years threatens attachment, causing problems for the child both in childhood and adulthood. Rutter (1981) observes that privation, rather than separation, is linked to severe consequences. Harlow's experiment (page 20) demonstrated the severe long-term effects of privation on infant monkeys. Since they are primates, similar effects would be expected in people but this cannot, ethically, be tested. Instead, evidence about the effects of privation in humans and whether these can be reversed comes from case studies of prived children.

Koluchová and the 'Czech twins'

Koluchová (1972, 1991) studied two severely abused twin boys. Their mother died and after a year in an institution, followed by six months with an aunt, they were raised by their stepmother who kept them locked in a dark closet and beat them. When the boys were found aged seven they were severely retarded, had no speech, and were afraid of adults, but were strongly attached to each other. After two years of hospital care (including physiotherapy, speech therapy and psychotherapy) they were fostered by a pair of sensitive and loving sisters. At 14 years old they had normal speech, social behaviour and IQ. At 20 both had above average IQ, were working and had romantic relationships.

Curtiss and the case of Genie

Curtiss (1977) studied a girl named 'Genie' who was discovered aged 13 having been severely abused and was almost entirely without speech. Her father believed she had learning difficulties so kept her isolated. She was beaten if she tried to communicate, having only basic interactions with her father and no one else. When rescued she was fostered first by a teacher and then by one of the psychologists studying her. She made progress, developing limited language and attachments to her carers. When the project funding ran out, Genie went into various foster-homes. She was physically abused again and regressed to the state she was in when first rescued. When briefly reunited with the psychologists, she showed great anger. Finally, Genie entered a stable foster-home.

Evaluating and comparing evidence from case studies of privation

As each case study is unique it is hard to make generalisations. However, in some ways the findings are similar. Both Genie and the Czech twins had virtually non-existent language and were too frightened of adults to form attachments initially.

Koluchová's findings suggest the effects of privation are reversible as the twins appear to have no long-term effects, but the evidence from Genie contradicts this as she remains severely affected. Several factors might account for these differences. Genie was older when found so had suffered more abuse, was further from any sensitive period than the twins and may have genuinely had learning difficulties. Perhaps most importantly, the twins had each other for both comfort and stimulation. Genie, in contrast, had no one.

2.10 Institutionalisation

Institutionalisation

Institutionalisation occurs when children spend a long time in an institution, such as a children's home. This experience is privation if they do not have the chance to form attachments or deprivation if they do, as the relationship may not be stable. Often, institutions contain a mixture of children who have experienced privation and deprivation, but institutionalisation has some distinctive patterns of attachment behaviour of its own (see page 29). Typically, children who go into care when young and who spend a long time there are disadvantaged in their development.

Studying institutionalisation

Hodges & Tizard (1989) compared the development of 65 children who entered institutional care when very young and either remained there, were adopted or were restored to their biological family. The children were assessed for social and emotional development at 4, 8 and 16 years using observations and interviews with teachers and carers. They found that at 4 and 8 years, the adopted group had fewest behavioural problems and were strongly attached to their carers. However, the adopted and restored children were attention seeking, suggesting disinhibited attachment (page 29). They were clingier and less likely to have developed close relationships. All three groups were aggressive and unpopular with their peers. By 16, the adoptees had entirely normal relationships with their adoptive families, but they still had problems with peer relationships. Being institutionalised as a baby had some long-term effects, regardless of whether infants were restored, adopted or stayed in institutions. Adoption, however, produced the best outcomes showing that the effects of privation are partially reversible. However, Rutter (1981) suggests that the child's experience prior to institutionalisation is also important. Those who are institutionalised because of parental illness or housing problems are better adjusted than children who have been abused or neglected. Since Hodges & Tizard's sample went into care very early the differences are more likely to be due to institutionalisation rather than their previous experiences.

Rutter *et al.* (1998) followed the progress of 111 Romanian orphans adopted in Britain. The children were initially developmentally delayed, underweight and about half showed signs of mental retardation. By four years old the children were similar to a control group of British children on both physical and intellectual development although the younger the child when adopted, the better they did. This suggests that good care can make up for very poor early institutional experiences.

 **Exam focus**

Distinguish between privation and institutionalisation.

(3 marks)

Zach's answer:

Privation is where a child doesn't have the chance to form an attachment at all, such as if they are neglected like Genie was. Institutionalisation is a pattern of attachment that happens because children in orphanages, etc, don't get one-to-one attention from the same carer so learn to grab attention from adults when they can. ②

 Examiner commentary

Zach has defined each term well but has not attempted to say how the two concepts are different, i.e. doesn't distinguish between them explicitly, so cannot access all the marks. He could have commented that children can become institutionalised even if they have previously formed an attachment or that the effects of institutionalisation seem to be relatively permanent whereas at least some of the effects of privation seem to be reversible.

Study note

Many researchers have investigated causes of failure to form attachments. These studies vary in terms of sample size, comparison groups, the age of the children at the start of the study, the length of time over which they were followed up, the measures of attachment and of adjustment and extraneous variables such as physical health. Using these basic ideas, you can evaluate any studies on privation and institutionalisation.

Disinhibited attachment

Research has shown that institutionalised children have a distinctive pattern of attachment behaviours called '**disinhibited attachment**'. They are clingy, attention seeking and are indiscriminate in their social interaction, i.e. their social behaviour is directed towards all adults rather than specific attachment figures. As they see many different carers (typically over 50 per week), and so little of any *one* carer, they cannot make their attachment behaviours exclusive. Children in care may also need to compete to be noticed, so attention seeking is understandable. Disinhibited attachment would therefore be an adaptive response to having multiple carers during the sensitive period (Rutter, 2006). Rutter *et al.* (2007) studied Romanian orphans who had been institutionalised then adopted. Even at 11 years their disinhibited attachment was still apparent and their age at adoption did not affect this behaviour. This suggests that they became institutionalised during the sensitive period when they experienced multiple carers early in life. Using the Strange Situation, Zeanah *et al.* (2005) found that many more Romanian children from institutions had insecure attachments compared to those who had never experienced institutionalisation. Few children in either group were Types A or C but many more of the institutionalisation group were Type D and 12.6 per cent of them behaved so oddly in the Strange Situation that their attachment types could not be classified.

Thinking psychologically

A number of different consequences of privation and institutionalisation have been described, these include: physical underdevelopment, lack of speech, fear of adults, attention seeking, disinhibited attachment, social problems, and intellectual underdevelopment.

Identify whether each idea is associated with privation, institutionalisation or both, which sources of evidence suggest this, and the extent to which each effect is reversible:

Table 2.3 Percentage of disinhibited attachments in institutionalised and control children (Zeanah *et al.*, 2005).

	% securely attached (Type B)	% disinhibited (Type D)
Institutionalised group	18.9	65.3
Control group	74	22

Exam focus

Evolutionary theories see secure attachments as functional, that is, of some benefit. Explain why the insecure attachments seen in cross-cultural studies and/ or studies of institutionalised children can be seen as functional in some way. *(4 marks)*

Mariah's answer:

X-cultural studies suggest that some cultures value independence but the SS measures attachments according to a US standard. Institutionalised children have D attachments because they don't have a main carer. ②

Examiner commentary

This is a demanding question at AS level. Mariah's answer is basically good but too brief (and using unexplained abbreviations is unwise). She could have expanded on which cultures value independence, the evidence for this and how it relates to insecure attachment. Alternatively (or additionally, as the question says 'and/ or') she could have said why disinhibited attachments might be functional, e.g. to help children with frequently changing carers to cope with being unable to form stable attachments.

2.11 Attachment in Everyday Life: day care

Day care and attachment theory

Day care is the most common cause of short-term separation. Economic and social reasons mean many children spend much of the week in day care. Bowlby's maternal deprivation hypothesis suggests that this separation from the main carer can disrupt the attachment process so damage the child's development. However, Bowlby studied longer-term separation and, as Rutter said, the worst effects are due to privation not deprivation.

Day care – the extended argument

The psychological arguments about day care–or at least long hours in it–are also used by some religious and politically right-wing groups to discourage mothers from working rather than out of concern for children's welfare. Others, including feminists wanting mothers to have the choice to work and governments avoiding unnecessary payments to non-working mothers, are interested in finding positive effects for children in day care.

Evidence for harmful effects on children's development

Belsky (1986) suggested that babies receiving day care in their first year (especially if this was full-time) had a higher risk of having insecure attachments and being aggressive than those cared for at home. Much research has supported this view, e.g. Bates *et al.* (1994) used teacher and peer-ratings of social behaviour in 600 American 5–6 year-olds. Children who had spent a lot of time in day care during their first five years were less socially skilled and less popular. Hofferth (1999) sampled 519 American children and found those spending long hours in day care were more aggressive.

Evidence for positive effects on children's development

There is less evidence to support this view although there is some. Andersson (1996) compared 128 Swedish children who had been in day care from infancy to 13 years with a control group who had had full-time maternal care. The day care group were judged to be more popular and socially skilled. Harrison & Ungerer (2002) studied 145 Australian mothers and their infants. Mothers who returned to work when their baby was less than five months old were the most likely to have babies classified as secure when assessed 12 months later using the Strange Situation. Having a job, commitment to work and feeling comfortable about using day care all predicted secure attachment.

There is a controversial idea that day care is good for children of poorer families as it is hard for them to give optimal care – implying that the middle classes make better parents so day care is good for one group of children but not for another. It is, however, supported by evidence. A meta-analysis (Ahnert *et al.*, 2006) found a strong positive correlation between socio-economic status and attachment security in children who did not have day care, but no link in those who did, supporting the idea that day care benefits poorer children.

Evaluating the evidence

Comparisons between children who experience day care and those who do not may not be valid as the children cannot be randomly allocated to 'day care' and 'no day care' conditions (they are not true experiments). Other differences between the groups could thus be causing the differences in behaviour. Koren-Karie (2001) compared 38 Israeli mothers who returned to work with a control group matched for age, income and their own attachment status. More mothers with insecure attachments themselves returned to work and used day care. Any effects on the day care group might therefore have been caused by the mothers' insecure attachments rather than by having day care.

Figure 2.9 Home care or day care: which is best?

Implications of research for day care practices

Research has shown that many factors influence the outcomes of day care for children. These include the age at which it starts, the time spent there, the quality and stability of the care, the management of the transition to day care and the child's initial attachment type.

Starting age and dose effects

Research suggests that entering day care prior to one year, rather than later day care such as pre-school nursery, is bad for children. Belsky (2002) explored the 'dose effect' – the amount of time spent in day care each day. In a study of 1083 American children he found those in day care for less than ten hours a week in their first 4½ years were five per cent more likely to be more aggressive than normal, but those having 30 hours or more had a 16 per cent greater chance of being aggressive. Ideally, therefore, children should start day care after age one year and not spend too long there per day.

The transition to day care

Ahnert *et al.* (2004) followed 70 German children under one year old from when they started day care for three months. Their Strange Situation responses showed that many children changed abruptly from secure to insecure attachment. When introduced to day care slowly, the secure babies stayed that way and some insecure babies became securely attached. This suggests that the stress of starting day care may be avoided by making the transition gradual, e.g. by having a parent there at first and staying for short periods. According to Belsky & Fearon (2002) this also depends on initial attachment type as only children with Type A attachments, not Types B or C, experience negative effects.

Figure 2.10 Earlier and longer day care is related to aggressive behaviour

Quality of day care

Allhusen *et al.* (2003) observed 985 children and their professional carers rating the carers for sensitive responsiveness, positive attitude towards the child and the amount of stimulation they provided. These measures showed that the better the quality of care, the greater the child's social competence and interactions with a friend and the lower their behavioural problems. This suggests that finding a facility offering a high quality of day care with enough positive, well-trained, simulating and sensitive staff is important. For example, Howes *et al.* (1998) followed up 36 American children in a nursery after sensitivity training was given to staff. This improved the sensitivity of some staff and the children these carers were responsible for were more likely to maintain or achieve a secure attachment.

Stability of day care

Research shows that a baby's attachment to its primary carer depends on months of regular contact and that having too many carers during a sensitive period can cause disinhibited attachment. To form secure attachments carers outside the home would therefore need the staff to be stable. A childminder provides a single figure with whom the child would have regular contact and Melhuish *et al.* (1990) found that children attending a childminder had higher rates of secure attachment, lower aggression and better peer relations than those in nurseries. In nurseries, a high ratio of staff to children would allow enough time with any one child to help to achieve consistency.

De Schipper *et al.* (2004) studied 186 children aged 6–30 months in nursery care. Use of the same nursery and regular contact with a key worker were both positively correlated with emotional well-being, whereas problem behaviour was associated with using several day care settings. This suggests that parents should provide stability by using the same day care facility and providers should keep staff turnover low (by offering good pay and conditions) and give each child a key worker with whom they have regular contact.

2.12 Developmental Psychology Summary

DEVELOPMENTAL PSYCHOLOGY

Developmental psychology looks at changes in thinking and behaviour over the lifespan, especially in childhood when many changes occur. **Attachment**, the formation of a strong bond between an infant and its carer, is an important aspect of these changes.

LEARNING THEORY AND ATTACHMENT

Classical conditioning makes babies associate the love of food with their carer and the **operant conditioning** explanation says that attachments are reinforced by their positive consequences (like food for babies and being smiled at for carers).

EVOLUTION AND ATTACHMENT

Evolutionary explanations say that attachment behaviours, such as **imprinting**, are innate and have arisen because they keep the young safe and allow them to learn.

Evaluating early explanations of attachment

Although there are opportunities for babies to learn to attach, this explanation is too simplistic. It cannot account for the level of emotion, why babies can attach to people who don't feed them, or why Harlow's monkeys preferred emotional comfort to food. Evolution can account for why attachments must form early (to ensure survival) and why they matter for later development in animals, which is also true in people (because it affects the ability to form stable adult relationships, including sexual relationships), but is also too simplistic to explain all aspects of human attachments.

BOWLBY'S THEORY OF ATTACHMENT

Monotropy suggests that an infant instinctively attaches to the main carer during a **critical period** and that this matters to later development. Children evoke responses from adults through **social releasers** and by signalling distress – behaviours which would evolve because they help survival. This first relationship becomes an **internal working model**; a pattern for future relationships.

Strengths of Bowlby's theory

Infants, including young monkeys, prefer comforting attachment figures (Harlow) and social processes, like **interactional synchrony**, matter; an unresponsive mother makes a baby distressed (Brazelton *et al.*). Evidence from monkeys (Harlow) and studies of imprinting (Lorenz) suggest attachment is innate as does the similarity of secure attachments across cultures (van IJzendoorn & Kroonenberg). Certainly attachment patterns transfer between generations as insecure mothers have insecure babies (Bailey *et al.*).

Weaknesses of Bowlby's theory

Evolutionary ideas are hard to test and animals may not be good models for human behaviour as we are more complex. Some evidence contradicts Bowlby, such as the formation of multiple attachments and cultural differences, suggesting some aspects of attachment are not innate (van IJzendoorn & Kroonenberg), as well as alternative explanations for differences in attachment such as infant temperament (Fuertes *et al.*).

Attachment types

Typically, Type B (secure) is the most common, followed by Type A (avoidant), then Type C (resistant). Main & Solomon identified Type D attachment, which combines types A and C.

The Strange Situation

Ainsworth & Wittig used the Strange Situation to classify attachment types. It measures proximity seeking, secure base behaviour, stranger anxiety, separation distress and the reuniting response.

Maternal sensitivity

Ainsworth suggested that **sensitive responsiveness** by the carer is needed for secure attachment. Without this, Type As become emotionally distant whereas Type Cs maintain close proximity and resist when reunited. Stayton & Ainsworth found that the babies of less sensitive mothers cried more. As adults, those who had secure attachments are more successful parents and have better friendships and romantic relationships (McCarthy).

Cultural variation in attachment

Van IJzendoorn & Kroonenberg found Type B attachment was the most common in all cultures and, except China, Japan and Israel, Type C the least. Germany had more Type C infants than other cultures. The variation within cultures was greater than between cultures. Differences may result from child-rearing practices (e.g. the value of independence in Germany) or reflect the validity of the Strange Situation across cultures (e.g. the response of Japanese mothers to separation). However, differences could be cultural if they evolved in response to differing environmental demands (Belsky).

DISRUPTION TO ATTACHMENT

Bowlby's maternal deprivation hypothesis suggests that separation for a child under two years can cause problems then and in adulthood. **Privation**, the failure to form an attachment, has more serious consequences than deprivation – the formation of an attachment which is temporarily broken.

Genie and the Czech twins

Curtiss found that Genie, discovered aged 13, recovered little from privation. She developed limited language and formed attachments to her carers, but then regressed when abused again. Koluchová found that the Czech twins, aged seven, recovered well from their abuse and privation. By age 14 they had normal language and by age 20 their IQs were above average and they had romantic relationships.

Is privation reversible?

In both case studies the individuals had no language and feared adults too much to attach initially. Koluchová's evidence suggests the effects of privation are reversible (as do Hodges & Tizard's findings for adopted children), but Genie's case contradicts this conclusion. The cases are, however, unique and age, the possibility that Genie had learning difficulties and that there were *two* twins, might account for the different outcomes, making generalisations difficult to draw.

INSTITUTIONALISATION

Children who spend a long time in **institutional** care may experience privation or deprivation and any attachments they form are transient. Hodges & Tizard found that children in care from a young age were typically disadvantaged, e.g. being aggressive and unpopular with peers. The subsequently adopted children had fewer behavioural problems (than those who remained in care or were restored to their biological family) and became attached to their new carers, although they and the restored children were clingy and attention seeking – suggesting disinhibited attachment.

Disinhibited attachment

As children in care may see many carers, their clingy, attention-seeking behaviour and indiscriminate social interaction can be seen as adaptive as they may need to compete to get noticed and cannot be exclusive in their attachment behaviours. Rutter *et al.* and Zeanah *et al.* found that institutionalised Romanian orphans who had then been adopted still had disinhibited attachment years later, suggesting that having multiple carers in the sensitive period irreversibly affects attachment.

DAY CARE

Day care causes short-term separation for many children so, according to Bowlby's theory, could disrupt attachment and damage development.

Negative implications for day care

Belsky suggested that babies in day care under one year old were at risk of insecure attachment and being aggressive. Bates *et al.* found that children under five spending a long time in day care were less socially skilled and less popular, and Hofferth found children spending long hours in day care were more aggressive.

Positive implications for day care

Andersson found children who had been in day care from infancy were more popular and socially skilled than those having full-time maternal care and Harrison & Ungerer found that the young babies of working mothers were likely to be securely attached at 12 months. Ahnert *et al.* showed that for children from low socio-economic status families (but not wealthier ones), the security of attachment was linked to day care suggesting – controversially – that day care benefits poorer children.

Evaluating the evidence

Comparisons between children in and not in day care may not be valid as the children cannot be randomly allocated to conditions. Pre-existing differences, such as insecurity of maternal attachments, could therefore be causing any differences in behaviour between those in day care or not (Koren-Karie).

What makes good day care?

Children should ideally not enter day care before one year of age nor spend too long there per day. Their introduction to the setting should be slow and accompanied by the main carers initially. A single, consistent setting should be chosen with sensitive staff and a low turnover. De Schipper *et al.* found that using the same nursery and having a key worker were linked to emotional well-being. Allhusen *et al.* found that children with day carers with high sensitive responsiveness had better social competence and fewer behavioural problems. Melhuish *et al.* found that children with a childminder were more likely to be securely attached, with good peer relations and low aggressiveness than those in nurseries.

2.13 Developmental Psychology Scenarios

Scenario 1: Jemima, Timothy and nursery choices

Bowlby's model of attachment

Jemima and Timothy are considering sending their two-year-old son to nursery. Jemima hates the thought as she feels that she never had a good relationship with her own mum because she had a string of nannies looking after her. Even Timothy admits that Jemima seems to find it hard to get on with people, even now.

Use your understanding of Bowlby's model of attachment to explain why Jemima doesn't have a good relationship with her mum and finds it hard to get on with people. Use research evidence to support your reasoning.

The effects of day care

Timothy's family have said that research evidence shows that nurseries are bad for children, making them aggressive and unable to get on with their peers, so they definitely shouldn't do it. But Jemima's best friend, Olga, knows that Jemima is finding being at home all the time depressing and although she's really tried she would probably be a better mum if she got out a bit now. Olga is German and thinks that English children are too protected and should be encouraged to socialise more anyway.

(a) Research has explored the effects of day care on aggression and peer relations. Referring to the text in both boxes above, use evidence to support either the argument of Timothy's family, or of Jemima's best friend.

(b) There are more cultural similarities than differences in attachment.' With reference to the text above and to research evidence, discuss this point of view.

Implications for childcare practices

Jemima and Timothy have decided to research some local childcare providers, but are not sure what they should be looking for.

Using evidence from research evidence, discuss the aspects of the facilities that they should consider to be important and why.

Revision note

It is useful to present information in as many different forms as you can to make yourself think. For this material you could use tables looking at:

- evidence for and against Bowlby's theory
- evidence about the positive and negative effects of day care or about the effects on peer relations, aggression and other aspects of social development
- ways that day care providers and parents can help children to cope with day care.

Scenario 2: Dan's attachment problems

Caring for Dan

Dan's parents both work abroad, travelling continuously, and his mother's pregnancy was very inconvenient. She came back to Britain to give birth then returned to work after ten weeks. Dan was moved to a new nursery each time they changed location until he was three years old and a place could be found for him in a boarding school with a nursery department. It was very strict and the children were discouraged from being sentimental. The boarding houses were run by all the school staff in rotation so the children didn't claim a particular member of staff for themselves. Dan saw his parents occasionally if they were in Britain for a meeting.

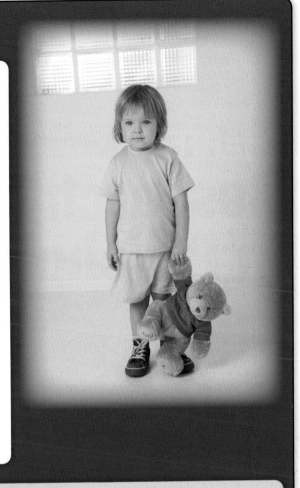

Using your understanding of attachment theory:

(a) Explain why a child might seek out a particular member of staff for themselves and why, given the opportunity, a member of staff might respond.

(b) Explain whether Dan will experience privation or deprivation as a result of his care, some possible effects of this experience and whether they are likely to be reversible.

(c) Dan may suffer from institutionalisation. What is institutionalisation and what are the consequences of it?

Assessing Dan

When Dan's parents pay a fleeting visit to see him one day they are accompanied by a psychologist who watches the way Dan responds to them and to her. She recognises some of the behaviours children exhibit in the Strange Situation.

(a) Describe the Strange Situation and what it measures.

(b) Referring to the scenario above, describe what kind of attachment behaviour Dan might exhibit and why.

Feeding Dan

In each of Dan's care environments he was well supplied with food. At school, he was always fed by the same few members of kitchen staff.

Describe the learning theory of attachment and use evidence to justify whether or not Dan would have formed an attachment to the kitchen staff at his school.

Study note

Look at some advertisements for day care providers in your local newspaper or on the Internet. Try to use ideas from developmental psychology to explain what they say. Can you think of anything to add to the adverts to make them better?

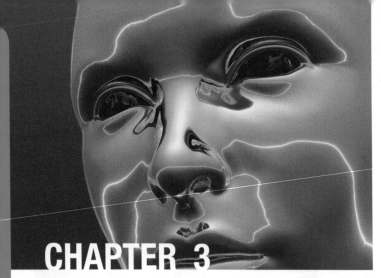

CHAPTER 3
Research Methods in Psychology

3.1 An Introduction to Research Methods

YOU NEED TO:

describe and evaluate these research methods:

- **experiments** (laboratory, field and natural)
- **self-reports** (including questionnaires and interviews)
- **observations** (naturalistic observation and using behavioural categories)
- **correlations**
- **case studies**

design studies using experiments, self-reports and observations, and understand and use:

- **aims and hypotheses** (directional and non-directional)
- **operationalisation of variables** (including independent and dependent variables)
- **pilot studies**
- **control of extraneous variables**
- **reliability and validity**
- **sampling techniques** (including random, opportunity and volunteer)
- **demand characteristics and investigator effects**

- **experimental designs** (repeated measures, independent groups and matched pairs)
- **ethical issues and BPS guidelines**

Analyse data, including:

- **quantitative data**
- **measures of central tendency** (mean, median, mode)
- **measures of dispersion** (range and standard deviation)
- **tables**
- **graphs**
- **scattergrams** (positive and negative correlations)
- **correlation coefficients**
- **qualitative data**
- **content analysis**

3.2 Qualitative and Quantitative Data and Content Analysis

Types of data

Quantitative data are numerical, like scores on a task or totals collected from experiments, correlations, questionnaires or observations using behavioural categories. Content analyses can also collect quantitative data. These data can be interpreted fairly easily with averages, measures of dispersion and graphs (pages 52–53) and are typically objective.

Qualitative data are descriptive, e.g. answers to open questions from self-reports (page 41) and detailed findings from observations and content analyses. They are harder to analyse as you need to look for general themes and interpretation can be subjective.

Revision note

To remember 'qualitative' and 'quantitative', think of the **qualities** of your best friend (i.e. **describe** them) and the **quantity** of friends you have (i.e. the **number** of them).

Quantitative data and levels of measurement

Quantitative data include **nominal** data (in named categories), e.g. the total number of children with childminders, in nursery or at home. Rating scales (e.g. words, numbers or points along a line) are **ordinal** scales, (e.g. 'Rate how well you get on with your parents') or **Likert scales** (e.g. 'Mothers should stay at home': *strongly agree, agree, don't know, disagree, strongly disagree*). **Interval** and **ratio** data (with equal gaps between the points) include standardised tests where each question is similar (interval) and scientific measurements like the age of a witness in years and months (ratio).

Revision note

To remember levels of measurement, think:
- nominal = 'name' or 'number'
- ordinal = order
- interval = equal intervals
- ratio = mathematical scales (like ratios in maths).

KEY TERMS

quantitative data numerical data from named categories or numerical scales

qualitative data descriptive data providing depth and detail

content analysis a technique for investigating information in material such as magazines, television programmes and transcripts of interviews which can produce quantitative or qualitative data

Qualitative data and content analysis

Content analysis is used to evaluate media, such as books and television. A sample is chosen (e.g. the type of book, how many and how much of each) and **coding units** (e.g. words or concepts) are operationally defined. Instances of each coding unit can be counted to produce quantitative data – this is readily analysed and replicated but is quite limited so may miss important ideas. Alternatively, descriptions can be analysed to produce qualitative data. Using **thematic analysis** a coding unit such as 'infant at home' might be categorised as 'positive'/'negative' or 'with mother'/'with father'. These themes can represent major or unusual ideas with examples. The categories may have been obvious to start with (pre-existing) or arise during the research (emergent). In interviews or case studies the latter can be identified through **collaborative research**, which uses feedback from participants to identify important themes, and examples are retained in full, e.g. as quotes, preserving the detail of the data.

Exam focus

Pair up each term on the left with **one or more** statements on the right.   *(3 marks)*

Quantitative data	Can always be simplified to numbers.
	Is detailed and in-depth.
Qualitative data	Is typically obtained in laboratory experiments.

Examiner commentary

The question says 'one or more' so you know there could be more than one line for each term. (Answers: Here, only the middle statement refers to qualitative data.)

3.3 Experimental Methods

Laboratory, field and natural experiments

An **experiment** has an **independent variable** (IV) and a **dependent variable** (DV). In a **true experiment** the researcher creates different conditions of the IV and measures changes in the DV. They also impose controls to limit extraneous variables — more so in lab experiments than those in the field (that is, where the participants would normally do the activity being tested). **Controls** help to ensure that changes in the IV are the only things that affect the DV, thus increasing **validity**. Lab experiments can also use **standardised procedures** — that are the same for each participant — which helps to make the procedure **reliable**. In a natural experiment the researcher cannot control the IV, but uses real differences or changes as the IV so measures the DV under different conditions. There is less control but the situation is more real (so findings are more likely to generalise beyond the experimental setting — high **ecological validity**). Each method has advantages and disadvantages (see Table 3.1).

Table 3.1 Strengths and weaknesses of experimental methods.

Method	Strengths	Weaknesses
Laboratory experiment	• Good control of **extraneous variables** • Causal relationships can be determined • Standard procedures allow replication improving reliability	• Artificial situations may make participants' behaviour unrepresentative • Participants may respond to **demand characteristics** and alter their behaviour • **Investigator effects** may bias results
Field experiment	• Participants in their normal situation are likely to behave in a representative way • Participants are likely to be unaware that they are in a study so demand characteristics will be less problematic	• Controlling extraneous variables is more difficult than in a lab so the researcher is less sure only the IV is affecting the DV • Fewer controls so harder to replicate than lab experiments • If participants are unaware that they are in a study this raises ethical issues
Natural experiment	• Can be used to study real-world issues • If participants are in their normal situation their behaviour is likely to be representative • Participants are likely to be unaware that they are in a study so demand characteristics will be less problematic • Used to investigate variables that could not practically or ethically be manipulated	• Only possible when naturally occurring differences arise • Control over extraneous variables is more difficult than in a lab experiment • The researcher is not manipulating the IV so is less sure that it is causing changes in the DV than in true experiments • Generally cannot be replicated

KEY TERMS

experiment a study in which an IV is manipulated and consequent changes in a DV are measured in order to establish a causes and effect relationship

independent variable the factor manipulated in an experiment

dependent variable the factor measured in an experiment

laboratory experiment a study in an artificial, controlled environment where the experimenter manipulates an IV and measures the DV

field experiment a study in which an IV is manipulated and DV measured in the participant's normal setting

natural experiment where an experimenter uses an existing difference as levels of an IV then measures the DV in each condition

control a way to standardise a procedure to avoid factors other than the IV affecting the DV so a cause-and-effect relationship can be established

validity the extent to which a test measures what it set out to measure

reliability the consistency of a measure, e.g. whether results from the same participants would be similar each time

extraneous variable a factor that could affect the DV and hide the effect of the IV

demand characteristics aspects of an experimental setting that indicate the aim to participants so change their behaviour

investigator effects influences a researcher has on the participants, e.g. by behaving differently to some participants, or expectations in interviews or observations

Experimental designs

There are three **experimental designs** (how participants are divided between levels of the IV). Participants may do all (**repeated measures**) or only one (**independent groups**) of the levels of the IV, or pairs can be divided so one goes into each group (**matched pairs**).

KEY TERMS

experimental design
the way in which participation in an experiment is organised. Participants can perform in only one or all of the levels of the IV

repeated measures design
each participant performs in every level of the IV

matched pairs design
participants are arranged into pairs that are similar in important ways for the study and one member of each pair performs in each level of the IV

independent groups design
different groups of participants are used in each level of the IV

Table 3.2 Strengths and weaknesses of experimental designs.

Design	Strengths	Weaknesses
Independent groups	• Different participants are used in each level of the IV so no order effects • Participants only see the experimental task once, reducing exposure to demand characteristics • The effects of individual differences can be reduced by random allocation to levels of the IV	• Individual differences may distort results if participants in one level of the IV differ from those in another • More participants are needed than with repeated measures (may be less ethical or hard to find)
Repeated measures	• Individual differences unlikely to distort the effect of the IV as participants do both levels • Counterbalancing reduces order effects • Uses fewer participants than repeated measures so is good when participants are hard to find • Blind procedures reduce demand characteristics	• Order effects and extraneous variables may distort the results • Participants see the experimental task more than once, increasing exposure to demand characteristics
Matched pairs	• Participants only see the experimental task once, reducing exposure to demand characteristics • Controls for individual differences, e.g. identical twins are excellent matched pairs • No order effects	• The similarity between pairs is limited by the matching process, which might be flawed • Matching participants is time-consuming and difficult

Exam focus

Zoë is doing an experiment on memory for neutral and sport-related words. She is worried that lots of sporty people might end up in one group so decides to test everyone on both kinds of words.

(a) What experimental design is Zoë using? *(1 mark)*

(b) What problems could Zoë encounter using this design? *(3 marks)*

(c) Choose one possible problem with the design and explain how Zoë could overcome it. *(2 marks)*

Jim's answer:

(a) Repeated groups. ①

(b) They might get muddled & recall the first list the second time, messing up the results. They might also get bored. ②

(c) Leave a big gap. ①

Examiner commentary

(a) This isn't quite right but 'repeated' makes it clear that he knows the design. Note that this answer doesn't even have to be a sentence.

(b) The first point is well made, the second only just says enough for another mark – boredom and confusion are two different reasons for a fatigue effect. Jim could also have described practice effects or demand characteristics.

(c) This is a very brief answer but is a possible solution. Jim hasn't *identified* the problem he is attempting to address but, fortunately for him, the examiner can work this out and award credit (a weak one mark). It is good to get into the habit of stating what you are addressing to increase your chances of getting credit. Describing counterbalancing or randomisation would have been alternative ways to earn marks.

Why use different experimental designs?

There are advantages and disadvantages to each design (see Table 3.2). If participants see the experimental setting more than once (i.e. in repeated measures) their second performance may be affected by **practice** or **fatigue** (**order effects**). These can be evened out by **counterbalancing**, so half the sample do the experimental conditions in one order and half in the opposite order. Alternatively, the orders can be **randomised**. Extraneous variables, such as noise during just one condition, can also distort the results.

Participants in independent groups designs are less likely to notice cues to the aims of the study, i.e. demand characteristics, so these are less likely to affect behaviour, increasing validity, compared to repeated measures designs. However, if participants in each condition happen to differ, differences in the DV may be due to **individual differences** (variation between people) rather than the IV. **Randomly allocating** participants to levels of the IV helps to avoid this but isn't always possible, e.g. in natural experiments. Matched pairs designs avoid all of these problems but are hard to do well as researchers must know in advance which variables to use to match participants and be able to find people who match in these ways.

To reduce the effects of demand characteristics, the participants' own level of the IV can be hidden (**single blind**). To reduce investigator effects, this can be hidden from the researchers interacting with the participants as well (**double blind**). This helps to overcome any unconscious influence the experimenters' expectations have on their behaviour towards the participants and therefore on the participants' performance.

 **Exam focus**

Two psychologists are investigating attachment using the Strange Situation. Dr Bishop compares the behaviour of ten babies with their mothers before and after each mother has stayed in hospital for a week for an operation. Dr Chan uses 20 pairs of mothers. Ten are asked to cuddle their babies much more than usual for a week, the others are not asked to do anything differently. At the end of the week, the behaviour of the babies with their mothers is measured.

(a) Identify the research methods being used by Dr Bishop and by Dr Chan. *(1 mark + 1 mark)*

(b) Identify the experimental designs being used by Dr Bishop and by Dr Chan. *(1 mark + 1 mark)*

(c) State one of these designs and describe two advantages of the design you have chosen. *(2 marks + 2 marks)*

Susan's answer:

(a) Dr Bishop is doing an experiment & Dr Chan is observing the babies. ①+⓪

(b) Dr Bishop is using repeated measures & Dr Chan is using independent variables. ①+⓪

(c) Dr Bishop's design is good because she can be sure that the differences between the babies are due to the mum being in hospital, not because the babies happen to be happy or miserable anyway. Also, Dr Bishop only needed 10 mum/baby pairs which is more ethical as fewer people were inconvenienced than in Dr Chan's experiment, so caused less psychological distress. ②+②

 Examiner commentary

(a) Susan is partly right; both are experiments but she needed to be more precise. Dr Bishop's is a natural experiment; Dr Chan's a lab experiment. Both are using observation to measure the DV but this is *not* the research method.

(b) Susan is right about Dr Bishop, but for Dr Chan the design is independent *groups*, the independent variable is the factor being manipulated.

(c) This is a good answer but it would have been safer to state the design, rather than 'Dr Bishop', in case her previous answer had been incorrect. Although the question didn't ask for the response to be contextualised, Susan has used the material well to explain her point so gains the marks anyway. If she had answered 'independent groups' ideas such as no risk of order effects, reduced effects of extraneous variables and demand characteristics would have been appropriate, though each would need to be expanded.

3.4 Self-Report Methods: interviews and questionnaires

Interviews and questionnaires

Self-report research methods are used to get first-hand information from participants about their thoughts or feelings. A **questionnaire** uses written questions and is **structured** (i.e. the order is fixed). The questions can be **closed** (a limited number of possible answers), e.g. 'Have you ever forgotten your own name?' or **open** (allowing freedom to give a longer, detailed answer), e.g. 'Describe the most important thing you have ever forgotten.'

Interviews can be structured (with fixed questions) or **unstructured**, where the interviewer decides which questions to ask and can follow a direction taken by the interviewee. They can also use a mixture of fixed and spontaneous questions (**semi-structured interview**). Like questionnaires, they can use closed or open questions. In reality, questionnaires tend to be used to collect lots of quantitative data using closed questions, which are relatively reliable and **objective**, but may not be very valid if they don't offer the participant the exact response they want to give. Interviews can collect more detailed, qualitative data with open questions and unstructured methods. This tends to be more valid as the interviewer can identify what is most important and the interviewee can express their ideas in their own words. However, the interpretation of these replies may be subjective and the possibility of the use of leading questions means the findings may be less valid.

Questionnaires and interviews can also be used to collect data for other research methods, for example a correlational analysis might make use of *questionnaire* data about the link between early trauma and later parenting ability. Similarly, *interviews* might be used with patients before and after brain operations to collect data for an experiment looking at the effect on memory. In these instances, self-report is being used as a research *technique* to measure variables for use in a different research method.

Thinking psychologically

Interviews are often used as a technique in case studies (page 47). Recall a case study of someone with amnesia. Why was it better to use an interview than a questionnaire?

Question types in questionnaires

There are several ways to elicit responses using closed questions:

- **Likert scales** ask the participant's opinion about a statement, e.g.:

  'Infants can attach to fathers as readily as to mothers.'
  strongly agree   agree   don't know   disagree   strongly disagree

- **Rating scales** ask the participant to choose a level on a continuum, e.g.:

  I get on with my mum:
  really well   1   2   3   4   5   6   7   *really badly*

  I get on with my dad:
  really well   1   2   3   4   5   6   7   *really badly*

- **Forced choice** questions give the participant limited options, e.g.:

  Babies are happiest when they are:

  (a) *Well fed*   (b) *Cuddled*

- **Semantic differentials** ask the participant to choose a point on a continuum, e.g.:

  As a parent, if you were separated from your child would you feel:

  confident _ *worried*

  tense _ *calm*

  sad _ *happy*

Table 3.3 Strengths and weaknesses of self-report techniques.

Self-report technique	Strengths	Weaknesses
Questionnaires	• Easy to send or email to participants so time and cost-efficient compared to interviewing each participant • Respondent may be more truthful on paper/online than face-to-face in an interview, especially if the questions are personal • Relatively easy to analyse quantitative data from closed questions compared to qualitative data from open questions	• Response biases such as always answering 'no' or always ticking the left-hand box can reduce validity • Limited because no flexibility for new questions to be added to allow collection of useful but unexpected data • Questionnaire return rates may be low and the sample may be biased
Interviews	• Structured interview data is relatively easy to analyse when quantitative as adding up numerical data is simpler than interpreting descriptions • Semi- or un-structured interviews let the researcher collect information that might be missed in structured techniques	• Structured interviews are limited by fixed questions • Investigator bias may reduce validity as expectations can alter the way questions are asked (affecting the respondents' answers) or the way the responses are interpreted
Both questionnaires and interviews	• Structured techniques can be easily repeated to generate more data or check findings • They can generate quantitative and/or qualitative data • Reliability between researchers can be improved with operationalisation and practice	• Participants may be affected by social desirability (responding as they think society expects) or leading questions • Only some people will be interviewed or fill in questionnaires so the sample may not represent the population well

Exam focus

Kelvin and Cynthia have written a questionnaire about student revision strategies.

(a) Identify a closed question in Kelvin and Cynthia's questionnaire and explain why it is a closed question. *(2 marks)*

(b) Identify an open question in Kelvin and Cynthia's questionnaire and explain why it is an open question. *(2 marks)*

(c) Which type of question, open or closed, collects qualitative data? *(1 mark)*

(d) Initially, Kelvin and Cynthia had planned to conduct an interview. Explain why it might have been better for them to use a questionnaire in this instance. *(6 marks)*

QUESTIONNAIRE

1. Which technique do you use most often (circle i, ii or iii):

   i) *Rereading your notes*

   ii) *Making up mnemonics*

   iii) *Answering past questions*

2. 'Last minute cramming is a good idea.'
   Circle the response that best fits your view:

   strongly agree   *disagree*   *agree*   *not sure*   *strongly disagree*

3. If there were no exams, just class assessment, how hard do you think you would work and why?

Alisha's answer:

(a) 1 because there are only three possible responses. ② (b) 3 as it asks for details about why. ② (c) Open. ① (d) They could ask lots more students because questionnaires take less time than other methods, so that would make their findings more reliable. It would also be more reliable because they would be sure that it was standardised whereas if some people were interviewed by Kelvin and some by Cynthia, they may have done it in different ways. The students might have lied about how hard they would really work just to be funny or because they were embarrassed to admit that they really would do some work without exams, so using questionnaires probably gave more honest & valid answers. ⑥

Examiner commentary

Alisha's answers are excellent if very brief. They are a good illustration of saving words (and therefore time) when they are not needed, e.g. in questions (a), (b) and (c), but writing in more detail where longer answers are required as in question (d).

3.5 Observations

Observations

Self-reports can only measure what a person *thinks* they would do, whereas **observations** allow researchers to record actual responses. This is especially important if the participants can't say what they would do, such as animals and children. For example, the Strange Situation tells us about a child's attachment *behaviours*; from this we can infer their attachment type.

Like self-reports, an observation can, however, be used either as a research method in its own right or as a technique for collecting data, for example as the DV in an experiment.

Naturalistic and controlled observations

Observations can either be conducted in the participant's own surroundings, such as in regular day care for a child (a **naturalistic observation**) or in a deliberately set-up situation (**controlled** or **contrived observation**). A naturalistic setting is likely to have higher validity, for example, an infant and mother are more likely to behave normally at home than in a new setting with different toys, noises and lights. A controlled setting, however, means the researcher can introduce changes, such as the mother's absence, the presence of a stranger or the appearance of another familiar figure. In a naturalistic setting the specific situations of interest may never arise and they are harder to control.

Both types of observation present ethical dilemmas. The intrusion caused by observers may be damaging if it disrupts an existing behaviour, such as attachment or a social or cognitive process, and if the participants are unaware of the observation, lack of informed consent is an issue.

KEY TERMS

observation a research method in which data collection is achieved by watching and recording the activity of people (or animals)

naturalistic observation the participant is watched in their own environment, i.e. in the normal place for the activity being observed

behavioural categories specific events in the participants' stream of activity which are independent and operationally defined

Observational techniques

Participants may be aware they are being observed (**disclosed**) or unaware (**non-disclosed**) and the observer may be part of the social group or activity (**participant**) or separate from it (**non-participant**). Non-disclosed observations raise the ethical issue of deception, whereas disclosed ones risk the effects of demand characteristics if the participants behave as they believe they are expected to. Non-participant observation can be conducted by videoing or with a hidden observer and is relatively objective compared to participant observation where emotional involvement in the situation can make the observer subjective.

In **non-focused observations** the observer records any behaviour they feel is relevant. This may be a starting point for a **focused observation**, to identify behaviours of interest for further study. To record specific behaviours the participants' stream of activity is broken into specific **behavioural categories**. These must be independent from each other and operationally defined. It is important that they can be seen rather than inferred, for example, in the Strange Situation 'proximity seeking' can be readily seen by the return of the child to the carer; 'distress' must be defined in terms of crying or other observable protests.

Table 3.4 Strengths and weaknesses of naturalistic observations.

Strengths	*Weaknesses*
• Behaviour is likely to be highly representative of real life, especially if non-disclosed, as it is seen in the normal setting so is better than self-reports, in which people may report their behaviour differently than they would actually do	• Participant observers may be biased if they become involved in the social situation
• In non-disclosed observations there is little risk of demand characteristics affecting behaviour	• **Inter-observer reliability** between multiple observers may be low, i.e. they may take different records from the same behaviours
• Data can be collected from participants who can't do self-reports or an experimental test, e.g. babies	• Non-disclosed observations raise ethical issues as participants are unaware they are being observed
• Can collect data when manipulation of a situation would be unethical or impractical	• Extraneous variables are harder to control than in controlled observations or lab experiments
• When behavioural categories are operationally defined, mutually exclusive and clearly observable, they are highly objective and reliable	• It can be difficult to separate a continuous stream of behaviour and to identify observable indicators of emotional states, reducing the reliability and validity of behavioural categories

Exam focus

Studies of babies' attachment behaviours conducted in their homes often use naturalistic observations.

(a) Describe naturalistic observation as a research method. *(4 marks)*
(b) Outline **one** strength and **one** weakness of naturalistic observations.
(2 marks + 2 marks)

Revision note

If you have time left over in the exam, remember that it is as important to reread the **question** as it is to reread your answer — be sure that you have answered the question set.

Martin's answer:

(a) Naturalistic observations can be focused or non-focused. They can also be disclosed or non-disclosed. The observer can either be part of the activity, like Curtiss was when she interacted with Genie, or they can be separate, like the observers who recorded the behaviour of mothers and babies in the Strange Situation. Observers use operationally defined behavioural categories to record which things the participants do. This is generally a list of the actions that can be seen, like cuddling or crying, rather than needing comfort or being unhappy, which can't be seen. The list is made out so that any activity only falls into one category. ④

(b) They are better than controlled observations because they are conducted in the participant's normal environment. This means they will be more likely to find behaviour that is representative of real life as they won't be affected so much as they would be if the setting was unfamiliar. ② Lab experiments generally have low mundane realism because they use tasks that aren't like real life and the findings won't apply to real life as they are done in a lab, so the ecological validity is low, but naturalistic experiments are done in real environments. ⓪

Examiner commentary

(a) Martin's answer starts off being just a list of terms which are relevant but are not explained at all so cannot earn him marks. He then more effectively describes the ideas of participant and non-participant observations and gives good elaboration using examples – this is much better writing. In the last section he uses the correct term and explains it – even better. Even though he has missed the essential element (where a naturalistic observation is conducted) his answer has ample relevant, accurate and detailed material for the full 4 marks.

(b) The first point Martin makes is a valid strength and is elaborated, so he gains 2 marks. The second point looks like a weakness, but the contrast shows that it is a weakness of lab experiments but a *strength* of naturalistic observations – so Martin hasn't answered the question and scores 0 for this part. He could have described the problems of reliability in naturalistic observations or of validity with the lack of controls.

Thinking psychologically

Many more experiments in social and developmental psychology use observation as a technique to measure the DV than in cognitive psychology or the investigation of individual differences. Why do you think this is the case?

Study note

The developmental psychology topic provides examples of all the key ideas from research methods. Try writing a list of the key terms in this chapter and illustrating each one with an example from a study investigating developmental psychology.

3.6 Correlations

Correlational analysis

The research method of **correlational analysis** investigates two variables measured on ordinal, interval or ratio scales to look for a relationship between them. It may be used to explore the possibility of a link between variables prior to experimental research or when it would be impractical or unethical to use an experimental method to manipulate variables. For example, it would be unethical to deliberately manipulate security of attachment to study the link between an individual's own attachment type and their children's.

Correlations and scattergrams

A **correlation** can be described in two ways: its *direction* and *strength*. In a **positive correlation** the two variables increase in the same direction – a high score on one is linked to a high score on the other. For example, the more sensitive responsiveness a mother shows, the more securely her infant is likely to be attached. In **negative correlations** the two variables increase in opposite directions – a high score on one is linked to a low score on the other. For example, more securely attached babies show less distress in the presence of strangers. Note that in neither case can a causal relationship be assumed; it might be that it's much easier to be sensitive towards securely attached babies or that both security of attachment and sensitivity are affected by some other factor.

These relationships can be illustrated using a **scattergram** on which each axis represents one of the variables. Each participant's scores are plotted as a single dot at the intersection of their score on each of the two variables. The line of best fit through these points indicates the direction of the relationship. A scattergram also shows the strength of the relationship – how closely linked the two variables are. If the correlation is strong the points will all lie close to the line of best fit (Figure 3.1a); if it is weak they will be more scattered (Figure 3.1b).

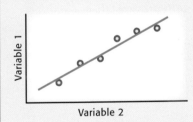

Figure 3.1a A strong positive correlation.

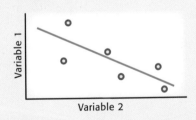

Figure 3.1b A weak negative correlation.

KEY TERMS

correlation a relationship between two measured variables such that a change in one variable is related to a change in the other

correlational analysis research method used to investigate a link between two measured variables

scattergram graph where data points represent scores on two measured variables

negative correlation a relationship between two variables where an increase in one accompanies a decrease in the other

positive correlation a relationship between two variables which increase together

correlation coefficient a mathematical measure showing the strength of a relationship between two variables
(+1 = perfect positive correlation, −1 = perfect negative correlation)

Table 3.5 Strengths and weaknesses of correlational analysis.

Strengths	**Weaknesses**
• A correlation can demonstrate the presence or absence of a relationship so is useful for indicating areas for subsequent experimental research. If there is a relationship, experimental research is worthwhile as a causal relationship might be found. If there is no correlational relationship it is unlikely that a causal relationship will be found in an experiment • A correlational study can be conducted on variables which can be measured but not manipulated, e.g. when experimentation would be impractical or unethical • It is possible to repeat the data collection for a correlational study so the findings can be verified	• A single correlational analysis cannot indicate whether a relationship is causal • If a correlational relationship is found this may be due to one of the measured variables or to another, unknown, variable • Correlational analysis can only be used with variables that can be measured on a scale (i.e. ordinal, interval or ratio data levels of measurement) • Any correlation found is limited by the reliability and validity of the tests used to measure the two variables

Correlation coefficients

A scattergram illustrates the strength and direction of a correlation, but a **correlation coefficient** measures these values exactly. If two variables are not correlated, they will have a coefficient of zero. A positive correlation is indicated by a value above zero up to +1, the strongest possible positive correlation. A negative correlation is indicated by a value between zero and -1, so -1 is the strongest possible negative correlation.

Thinking psychologically

Erickson *et al.* (2010) found a positive correlation between the volume of some brain areas and how well participants learned to play the video game Space Fortress. Interestingly, they did not find a relationship between hippocampal volume and learning (although the volume of two areas of the striatum was related to different learning). The striatum is known to be involved in the acquisition of procedural memories. As the hippocampus has been linked to spatial memory (as well as transfer from STM to LTM) what predictions could you make about video games that might relate to hippocampal volume?

Figure 3.2
A view from the specially designed game Space Fortress, in which participants have to avoid various dangers to their own spaceship whilst trying to destroy a fortress.

Exam focus

Indicate whether each relationship described below is a positive or a negative correlation by ticking **one** box only on each line. *(3 marks)*

	Positive	Negative
1. The more anxious people are, the less accurate their eyewitness testimonies.		
2. People who are more securely attached as infants have more strongly attached children.		
3. The less time you spend rehearsing a memory, the worse your recall.		

Revision note

If you can't remember which way round the lines go on positive and negative correlations, think of an upper case N for negative — the middle bar slopes the same way as the line on a scattergram for a negative correlation.

Sharon's answer:

	Positive	Negative
1.	✔	✔
2.	✔	✔
3.	✔	✔

Sharon ticked all six boxes. ⓪

Examiner commentary

If you tick more than the required number of boxes your answer will earn no marks at all.
(Answers: 1 negative, 2 positive, 3 positive.
Note that in the last statement the two variables are going down *together*, so it is a positive correlation.)

Exam focus

Habib and Dave both do a correlational analysis but get different results. Habib gets a correlational coefficient of +0.4 and Dave gets a correlational coefficient of -0.5. Who has the strongest correlation? *(1 mark)*

Valerie's answer:

Habib, because his is a plus number. ⓪

Examiner commentary

The correct answer is Dave. Valerie didn't need to explain her answer as the question only asks which is stronger, but the reason is because 0.5 is bigger than 0.4. It doesn't matter about the sign, this simply tells you whether it is a positive or negative correlation.

3.7 Case Studies

What's different about a case study?

Unlike other methods, a **case study** focuses on just one person (or a single 'instance', e.g. a family). They are studied in-depth using a range of techniques such as observations, interviews and tests. The reason for conducting research in most investigations is to find out something new. Case studies, in contrast, are often exploring something that has already happened, such as the consequences of privation or amnesia. These instances are generally unusual, so another difference is that they investigate atypical examples – therefore generalisation is often difficult. Importantly, they offer the chance to explore events that it would be unethical to produce experimentally. Finally, the primary aim may not be research but therapy – the psychologist records the evidence they find as they help a client.

KEY TERMS

case study an investigation of one person in detail using techniques such as interviewing, observation and conducting tests

How is a case study conducted?

The nature of the research will depend on the case and the investigator's psychological perspective. A developmental psychologist exploring a parent reunited with their child after a long period of separation might observe their behaviours, interview the adult to investigate their feelings and use questionnaires to find out about their child's experiences. In contrast, a cognitive psychologist investigating a patient with amnesia is likely to use tests of current ability and compare these to a non-impaired standard.

Table 3.6 Strengths and weaknesses of case studies.

Strengths	Weaknesses
• Case studies provide rich, in-depth data which give more detailed information than can be obtained through methods such as experiments • Unusual instances, which could be overlooked in averaged data from experiments, are preserved • Rare cases offer opportunities to study situations that could not – ethically or practically – be artificially contrived • The realistic context of an individual's life or other unique instance allow for the investigation of the complex interaction of many factors • Using many different sources of information from a range of techniques allows researchers to verify findings and be more certain about them	• Each case study is a unique investigation of a single situation or individual so the findings may not generalise to others • Case studies investigate rare individuals so they may be readily identifiable – an ethical issue • The evidence obtained from an individual that relates to the past may be hard to verify • An investigator may get to know the individual well so may lose objectivity • Variables cannot be controlled so causal relationships cannot be investigated • The theoretical perspective of the investigator may cause them to interpret their findings in a biased way so they may tend to find what they wish to find or believe to be true

Exam focus

(a) Outline **two** strengths of the case study method.

(2 marks + 2 marks)

(b) Outline **two** weaknesses of the case study method.

(2 marks + 2 marks)

Beverley's answer:

(a) The case study is a good method because it looks at a single person producing lots of descriptive, qualitative data from different sources – like brain scans and IQ tests – which can be used for finding out new information and supporting existing theories. ⓪

(b) The case study is a bad method because experiments, correlations or self-reports are better. ⓪

Examiner commentary

These are difficult questions because they ask for two, rather than just one, evaluative point. In both (a) and (b) Beverley sounds like she knows what she is doing because the answers start well with

'The case study is a good/bad method because...'

Unfortunately, she then offers description rather than evaluation. She doesn't give any reasoning to support her view and that is what would earn marks. Beverley also only suggests one idea (she possibly misread the question); she needed to give two strengths for (a) and two weaknesses for (b). Any advantages or disadvantages of case studies compared to other methods, e.g. from Table 3.6, would have been creditworthy.

3.8 Selecting Methods and Designing Studies

Aims and hypotheses

All investigations have an **aim** and some express the predicted outcome as a **hypothesis** – a testable statement. Hypotheses can either predict that 'there will be an effect' – a **non-directional hypothesis** – or that 'the effect will go a particular way' – a **directional hypothesis**.

Non-directional hypotheses in experiments are of the general form 'There will be a difference in *the DV* between *the levels of the IV*', e.g. 'There will be a difference in *proximity seeking* between *infants with sensitive and insensitive mothers*'. In correlations they take the general form 'There will be a relationship between *one variable* and *the other variable*', e.g. 'There will be a relationship between *age* and *accuracy of eyewitness testimony*'.

Directional hypotheses in experiments take the general form '*The DV* will be bigger in *one level of the IV* than in *the other level of the IV*', although there are many different ways to express this. For example, '*Proximity seeking* will be greater in *insecurely attached infants* than in *securely attached infants*'. In correlations they take the form, 'There will be a *positive/negative* correlation between *one variable* and *the other variable*', although again this can be expressed differently. For example, 'There will be a *negative correlation* between *age* and *accuracy of eyewitness testimony*'.

Operationalising variables

Any variable needs to be defined to ensure it is a valid manipulation or measure (**operationalisation**) and to aid replication, e.g. a DV of 'security of attachment' could be defined by an infant's responses in the Strange Situation. In a memory study the DV could be defined by the number of words recalled and the IV of 'amount of rehearsal' as the time allowed for learning.

Exam focus

Identify whether each hypothesis is a directional or non-directional hypothesis and whether it relates to an experiment or correlation. *(3 marks)*

	Directional or non-directional	Experimental or correlational
1. Memory will be worse after a delay than for immediate recall.		
2. Child and adult witnesses differ in accuracy of their testimonies.		
3. Children spending longer in day care are more aggressive.		

Examiner commentary

Note that you will need to be able to write hypotheses too. (Answers: 1 directional and experimental, 2 non-directional and experimental, 3 directional and correlational.)

Study note

When writing experimental hypotheses, include the IV and the DV, saying which level of the IV will be 'better' in terms of the DV if it is directional. This will help you to avoid saying 'There will be a difference between the IV and the DV' – which is a nonsense statement.

Pilot studies – what to look for

The aim of a **pilot study** is to check the method (not to see if the results are what was expected) and find solutions to any issues. This ensures high reliability and validity.

In experiments it is important to check:

- the participants can follow the **standardised instructions**
- that the apparatus and materials are appropriate
- that the DV covers the full range of scores (to avoid **floor** or **ceiling effects**)
- for any possible extraneous variables that need to be controlled
- whether any aspects of the procedure will lead to demand characteristics
- whether there are any order effects in a repeated measures design.

In self-reports it is important to check:

- that the participants understand the questions and are prepared to answer them
- that closed questions offer suitable options
- whether open questions are also needed to elicit unpredictable responses
- that response biases are limited, e.g. through the use of **filler questions** and reversal of positive and negative 'ends' of Likert scales and semantic differentials
- whether the reporting method is appropriate, e.g. if a face-to-face interview is too intimidating should it be changed to a questionnaire?

In observations it is important to check:

- that observers agree on operational definitions of behavioural categories
- inter-observer reliability – do they need practice?
- that the behavioural categories include all the important behaviours
- that the behavioural categories do not overlap
- whether the participants are affected by the observers – should they be non-disclosed?

Exam focus

Lucy and Quentin are going to conduct studies on memory. They are both interested in how much people forget and what cues they use to help them remember. Lucy decides she will do a lab experiment comparing recall with visual or verbal cues. Quentin opts for a questionnaire. He too investigates visual and verbal cues.

Choose **either** Lucy's lab experiment **or** Quentin's questionnaire to answer both questions (a) and (b).

(a) Identify **two** factors that will need to be operationally defined in the proposed study and suggest possible definitions.

(2 marks + 2 marks)

(b) Outline **two** ways in which a pilot study could help to improve the proposed study. *(2 marks + 2 marks)*

Franky's answer:

(a) Lucy should operationalise the IV as visual, e.g. typed words on cards in the same font and size, or verbal, e.g. words spoken at a fixed volume and rate and the DV of recall. ②+①

(b) Quentin should use his pilot study to decide whether to use filler questions. They could help make the questionnaire more valid if people guess the purpose and all give predictable answers. Also if he needs open questions to get detailed answers if closed questions are too limiting. ②+②

Examiner commentary

Franky has written good answers to both (a) and (b) but only his answer to (b) counts as he has not followed the either/or instruction (and his answer to (b) is best). If the answer to (a) had counted, he would have earned 3 marks and could have earned the last mark for saying how Lucy could define recall.

The British Psychological Society guidelines in summary

- **Informed consent**: participants should know what they are agreeing to and give *real* consent.
- **Deception**: this should be avoided. If deceived, participants should be told the real aim of the study as soon as possible.
- **Debriefing**: when participants know they have participated in a study they should get an explanation quickly and should leave in at least as positive a mood as they started.
- **Withdrawal**: participants should be told they can leave the study at any point, regardless of payment, and be allowed to withdraw their data.
- **Confidentiality**: unless agreed with participants in advance, individual results and personal information about them should remain secret and safe.
- **Protection**: participants should not be exposed to any physical or psychological harm (greater than they would encounter in their usual lifestyle).
- **Privacy in observations**: privacy should not be invaded. If observation is non-disclosed it should only be done where participants would expect to be watched.

Thinking psychologically

Godden & Baddeley (1975) used trained divers, Smythe & Costall (2003) used students, Scoville & Milner (1957) described an amnesic patient, Curtiss (1977) described Genie, and Donovan *et al.* (2007) explored allegedly insensitive mothers. What ethical issues did each research project face and how did they solve these issues?

In Krackow & Lynn's (2003) experiment children were asked about being touched on the bottom (which didn't happen). The parents were told about the question and some removed their children. What ethical issues were raised and how were they dealt with?

Solving ethical issues

All psychological research raises some ethical issues. These issues must be identified and resolved before the research commences. If issues arise once research has begun it should be stopped. Table 3.7 suggests ways to tackle common **ethical issues**.

> **Study note**
>
> Most of the guidelines are also issues, but debriefing is just a *solution* not a problem. However, the latest version of the BPS Ethical Principles (September 2009) does recognise the failure to debrief as an issue — so it may be acceptable in the future.

Table 3.7 Ethical issues and possible ways to resolve them.

Issue	Possible solutions
Consent	Give a full brief to participants so they can give informed consent. If this would jeopardise the validity of the study they can be offered the right to withdraw or **presumptive consent** can be gained (by asking a similar group if they would object to the procedure).
Deception	As this should be avoided, senior colleagues or an ethical committee should weigh up the costs to participants compared to the possible benefits of findings. If the study goes ahead, participants should be fully debriefed immediately after and allowed to withdraw their results.
Withdrawal	Tell participants at the start of the study that they have the right to leave and that this is not dependent on any payment. Remind them if necessary later in the study.
Confidentiality	Participants' names should not be recorded or, if essential for contacting them again, should be stored separately from their data. Numbers or pseudonyms should be used instead.
Protection	The procedure should be safe for participants. If physical dangers are possible, participants skilled and experienced in dealing with them should be recruited so they are under no greater risk than normal. If unexpected risks arise the study should be stopped.
Privacy	Observations should only be done in public places, not where people expect to be in private. Participants can be asked afterwards for their **retrospective consent** or allowed to withdraw their data.

> **Study note**
>
> Look back through the studies you have learned about. Find examples where the researchers clearly have, or have not, followed each of the guidelines in Table 3.7.

Sampling techniques

A **population** is a target group of people, such as 'parents using day care in the London area'. The **sample** are the people selected from this group who become participants. The **sampling technique** is the method used to find this sample. There are several ways to make this selection and they differ in the extent to which the sample is representative, i.e. whether it is likely to be typical of the population. These are described, with their advantages and disadvantages, in Table 3.8.

KEY TERMS

sampling technique the way in which the group of participants (the sample) is selected from the population

opportunity sampling selecting participants according to availability

random sampling selecting participants such that each member of a population has an equal chance of being chosen

volunteer sampling this is a way to recruit people through advertising – the participants respond to a request rather than being approached by the experimenter

Table 3.8 Sampling techniques and their strengths and weaknesses.

Technique	Advantages	Disadvantages
Opportunity sampling – participants are chosen because they are available, e.g. university students selected because they are around at the time	Quicker and easier than other methods as the participants are readily available	Non-representative as the kinds of people available are likely to be limited, and therefore similar, making the sample biased
Random sampling – all members of the population (i.e. possible participants) are allocated numbers and a fixed amount of these are selected in a unbiased way, e.g. by taking numbers from a hat or using a random number generator	Should be representative as all types of people in the population are equally likely to be chosen	Difficult as everyone in the population must be equally likely to be chosen but this is hard to achieve, e.g. through lack of information or access and even then the sample may be biased, e.g. if only girls happen to be selected
Volunteer sampling – participants are invited to participate, e.g. through advertisements via email or notices: those who reply become the sample	Relatively easy because the participants come to you and are committed, e.g. likely to turn up for repeat testing	Non-representative as the kinds of people who respond to requests are likely to be similar, e.g. better educated or have free time

Exam focus

Harry and Eloise are studying working memory using sound-based, visual and spatial tests. They know working memory is affected by many factors and want to avoid differences between participants affecting the results. They have already decided to do a repeated measures design and are wondering which sampling technique they should use.

(a) Describe **two** possible sampling techniques they could use.

(2 marks + 2 marks)

(b) Justify which sampling technique would be better for Harry and Eloise to use.

(2 marks)

Study note

You can't just say opportunity sampling is 'quick and easy', you must say compared to what. Similarly, simply saying 'random samples are representative' wouldn't get credit, you need to explain why, i.e. because all members of the population are equally likely to be selected.

Leah's answer:

(a) *Random sampling is where people are chosen because they just happen to be there when the study is being done.* ⓪ *You get a volunteer sample by giving people the chance to offer to take part, like by putting requests into letterboxes so people can choose to ignore it or come along to the study.* ②

(b) *Random sampling because it's more likely to give an unbiased sample as the volunteers might all be similar and are often better educated so might have better memories.* ②

Examiner commentary

(a) This starts off defining opportunity sampling – a common mistake. Remember that random sampling is about an equal chance of any person being selected.

(b) This is a good answer and earns marks even though (a) was incorrect.

3.9 Descriptive Statistics for Quantitative Data

Measures of central tendency

To illustrate a 'typical' score in a set of numerical data, a **measure of central tendency** is used. There are three different ones because some are more informative, but cannot be used on all levels of measurement (see page 37).

The mode is the most frequent score(s) in a set of results – there can be more than one mode. If 50 families report their day care practices and 19 say 'at home', 8 say 'with a childminder', 4 say 'with another carer' and 19 say 'in a nursery' the modal care arrangements would be 'at home' and 'in a nursery'.

The median is the middle score when the data are in rank order. When the group has an even number of scores the two numbers in the middle are added together and divided by two to find the median. A questionnaire on forgetting asks the question 'Rate how bothered you are about not remembering someone's name' offering a scale of 1–9. Ten participants give the following scores: 7, 9, 3, 2, 6, 7, 1, 5, 4, 3. In rank order the list becomes: 1, 2, 3, 3, 4, 5, 6, 7, 7, 9. The middle numbers are 4 and 5 so 4 plus 5, divided by 2, gives a median of 4.5.

The mean is worked out by adding up all the scores and dividing by the number of scores (including zero scores). A memory test produces this set of 10 scores: 5, 8, 7, 10, 7, 2, 10, 3, 3, 5. Adding the scores together gives a total of 60, divided by 10 gives a mean score of 6.

KEY TERMS

measure of central tendency
a mathematical way to describe a typical or average score from a data set (such as using the mode, median or mean)

measure of dispersion
a mathematical way to describe how spread out the scores in a data set are (such as the range and standard deviation)

range a measure of spread calculated as the difference between the smallest and the largest score in a data set

standard deviation a measure of spread calculated as the average variation either side of the mean

Table 3.9 Measures of central tendency and their strengths and weaknesses.

Measure of central tendency	Advantages	Disadvantages
Mode	• Can be used with any level of measurement • Not affected by extreme scores	• Not very informative • Ignores most of the data
Median	• Can be used with ordinal, interval and ratio data • Not affected by extreme scores	• Not as informative as the mean • Does not take all the scores into account
Mean	• The most informative measure as it takes every score into account	• Can only be used with interval or ratio data • Can be affected by extreme scores

Measures of dispersion

A **measure of dispersion** describes how spread out the scores are within the set. Two ways to illustrate this are the range and the standard deviation.

The **range** is the difference between the smallest and the largest score. In a test of proximity seeking, the greatest distance each child moved from his or her mother was measured. The distances (in metres) were 1.5, 1.8, 4, 2.2, 1.5, 1. The range is 3 (1 to 4). It is simple to work out and relates directly to actual scores, but it doesn't take the value of every score into account and can be misleading if there is even one extreme score.

The **standard deviation** calculates the average variation either side of the mean. More variation produces a larger standard deviation. For the set of distances above, the mean is 2 and standard deviation is 1.06. Compare these to this set of distances for another group of children in the same test: 0.5, 0.7, 2.1, 4.3, 0.9, 3.5. Again, the mean is 2, but the standard deviation is 1.59. It is bigger because the scores in this set are more spread out. The standard deviation is complex to calculate but is more informative than the range as it is based on every single score. However, the importance of odd, very large or small scores may be hidden.

Revision note

Remember the measures of central tendency as:
- <u>mode</u> = <u>most</u> common
- <u>median</u> = <u>mid</u>dle
- mean you probably already know as the 'average'.

Tables

The **raw data** (the scores collected in a study) are generally summarised using totals or percentages and measures of central tendency and spread. The raw data, or a summary, can be displayed in a table. This should have a title and each row and column should have a heading. If there are units, these should be written once in the heading, not in each 'cell'.

Bar charts

A bar chart (with *separate* bars) is used when the data is in discrete categories, e.g. for the totals of nominal data and for comparing measures of central tendency (modes, medians or means) for each level of the IV in an experiment. For experimental results the levels of the IV go along the *x* axis and the DV up the *y* axis. These should each have an axis label and any units should be given.

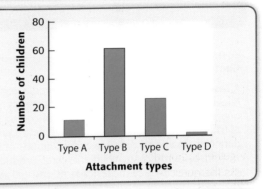

Figure 3.2 Number of children of each attachment type.

Histograms and frequency distributions

A histogram is used to illustrate continuous data, e.g. to show the distribution of a set of scores. The scale of the DV is plotted along the *x* axis and the frequency of each score is plotted up the *y* axis. The scores on the *x* axis may be in categories but because these are adjacent on a scale, rather than entirely separate measures, the bars are drawn next to each other. A frequency distribution is plotted on similar axes but points marking the frequency of each score are joined up to form a line.

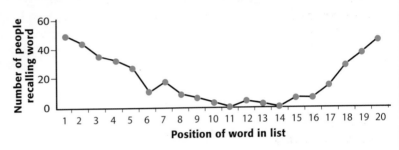

Figure 3.3 Serial position curve.

Exam focus

Two students want to know which measure of central tendency to use on their data.

(a) (i) Rashid measured the heart rate of infants during the separation phase of the Strange Situation to see how stressed they were. Which measure of central tendency should he use and why? *(2 marks)*

(ii) Gary asked adults about their own childhoods to find out whether their parents were strict, obsessive, fair or negligent. Which measure of central tendency should he use and why? *(2 marks)*

(b) Identify **one** strength and **one** weakness of using standard deviation. *(1 mark + 1 mark)*

Scott's answer:

(a) (i) He should use the median because it can be used on ratio data like beats per minute. ⓪

(ii) The words are on a scale but the gaps are uneven so he has to use the median, which is better than the mode as it tells you more, but less good than the mean as it doesn't use every number. ⓪

(b) Good as takes every score into account, bad because it doesn't identify extreme data points. ①+①

Examiner commentary
(a) (i) Rashid ought to use the mean (for the reason Scott gives) but as 'median' is not the best choice and Scott's justification does not match his suggestion, he scores 0.
(a) (ii) If the words had been on a scale, Scott's answer would have been correct but they aren't – they are nominal categories – so the answer should have been the mode.
(b) A brief but good answer –·which is all that is required for a 1+1 mark allocation.

3.10 Research Methods in Psychology Summary

TYPES OF DATA

Quantitative data are numerical and typically objective whereas **qualitative** data are descriptive and may be subjective. Quantitative data can come from nominal, ordinal, interval or ratio levels of measurement, nominal (categories) being the least, and ratio (mathematical scales) the most, informative.

Content analysis

A research method used to analyse media, e.g. television. A sample is chosen and coding units operationalised. Counting examples of coding units, e.g. of 'child crying' produces quantitative data. Qualitative data can also be recorded, e.g. descriptions of the responses of the crying child and carer, producing detailed examples of major ideas or unusual events.

Presenting qualitative data

Descriptive findings from content analyses (and from open questions in self-reports) can be presented using thematic analysis. Pre-existing or emergent categories represent key themes in the data. In interviews or case studies collaboration with participants can help to identify important themes and detail is preserved, e.g. as quotations.

EXPERIMENTS

In true – **laboratory** or **field** – **experiments**, the DV is measured to investigate the effect of the manipulation of the IV. In a **natural experiment** the IV is created by pre-existing differences or changes so the DV is measured in different conditions.

Strengths of experiments

Lab experiments have high validity as they can **control extraneous variables** (so causal relationships can be established) and standardised procedures increase reliability. Field experiments may have higher ecological validity as the participants are in the normal environment for the activity being studied and there are fewer **demand characteristics** if they are unaware they are in a study. Natural experiments have similar advantages to field studies, but also allow the investigation of variables that cannot be manipulated.

Weaknesses of experiments

A lab is an artificial setting so behaviour may be unrepresentative and demand characteristics may alter participants' behaviour. In field and natural experiments, extraneous variables are harder to control and if participants are unaware that they are in a study, this raises ethical issues. In natural experiments researchers can be less sure of causal effects and cannot replicate their findings.

EXPERIMENTAL DESIGNS

Participants are divided between levels of the IV. In **repeated measures** the same participants do all levels; in **independent groups** different participants do each level. In **matched pairs** individuals who are similar are divided up so one participant is in each level.

Strengths of repeated measures designs

The effects of individual differences are minimal and fewer participants are needed than in other designs. Counterbalancing can reduce order effects and blind procedures can reduce the influence of demand characteristics.

Strengths of independent groups designs

Order effects do not arise and demand characteristics are less problematic than in repeated measures designs. The effects of individual differences can be reduced by random allocation to levels of the IV.

Strengths of matched pairs designs

Order effects do not arise. Demand characteristics are less problematic than in repeated measures designs and the effects of individual differences are reduced compared to other designs.

Weaknesses of repeated measures designs

Order effects and demand characteristics can be problematic.

Weaknesses of independent groups designs

Individual differences can be problematic. More participants are needed than in a repeated measures design, which may present an ethical or practical problem.

Weaknesses of matched pairs designs

Matching participants is difficult and individual differences may be problematic if matching is flawed.

SELF-REPORTS

Interviews (face-to-face) and **questionnaires** (written) are used to get information from participants by **self-report**. Open or closed questions are asked, the former commonly in unstructured interviews and the latter in structured interviews and questionnaires. Closed questions produce quantitative data and include Likert scales, rating scales and forced choice questions. Qualitative data is collected using open questions such as, 'What do you think about day care?'

Strengths of questionnaires

They can generate qualitative or quantitative data and can be replicated. They are easy to distribute so a large group can be targeted and the large volume of data from closed questions is easy to analyse. Respondents may be more truthful than when face-to-face.

Strengths of interviews

They can generate qualitative or quantitative data and structured interviews can be replicated. Quantitative data from closed questions is easy to analyse. Unstructured interviews allow new questions to collect data that could otherwise be missed.

Weaknesses of questionnaires

Social desirability, leading questions and an inflexible question set can limit the validity of the data. Return rates may be low and can produce a sampling bias. Response biases can reduce the validity of results.

Weaknesses of interviews

Social desirability and leading questions reduce the validity of the data as can the limited questions in structured interviews. Investigator bias may reduce validity in unstructured interviews. A sampling bias arises if only some types of people will be interviewed.

OBSERVATION

This can be used as a research method or to collect data for an experiment or correlational analysis. **Naturalistic observations** are done in the participant's own, unchanged, surroundings. In controlled observations, the researcher introduces changes such as in the Strange Situation.

Observational techniques

In disclosed observations participants know they are being watched whereas in non-disclosed ones, they do not. When 'participant' the observer is part of the activity being observed, when 'non-participant' they are not. In non-focused observations any relevant behaviours are recorded. Focused observations are limited to specific **behavioural categories**.

Strengths of observational techniques

Data can be collected from participants who cannot be tested in other ways (e.g. babies) and when manipulation is unethical or impractical. Naturalistic observations, especially when non-disclosed, produce valid reports of behaviour. Mutually exclusive, operationally defined behavioural categories are objective and reliable.

Weaknesses of observational techniques

Participant observers may become subjective and non-disclosed observations raise ethical issues. Inter-observer reliability may be low and difficulty distinguishing behaviours may lower the validity and reliability of behavioural categories. In naturalistic observations extraneous variables are hard to control.

CORRELATIONAL ANALYSIS

This looks for a relationship between two measured variables either as a prelude to experimental research or as a research method when it is impractical or unethical to manipulate variables.

Scattergrams and correlation coefficients

In a **positive correlation** both variables increase in the same direction. The **correlation coefficient** – a measure of the strength of the relationship – will be between 0 and +1. In a **negative correlation** the variables increase in opposite directions (with a coefficient between 0 and -1). A scattergram represents the two scores from each participant along the *x* and *y* axes of a graph as a single point. A line through these points shows the direction of the correlation. Widely spread points indicate a weak correlation (with a coefficient nearer to zero). When most points fall close to the line the correlation is strong (with a coefficient nearer to +1 or to -1).

Strengths of studies using correlational analysis

These can look for relationships to decide if experimental work is worthwhile or to investigate variables that cannot practically or ethically be manipulated. Data collection can be replicated to verify findings.

Weaknesses of studies using correlational analysis

A single correlation cannot establish a causal relationship and any link identified could be caused by a different variable from those being measured. Findings from correlational analysis are only as valid and reliable as the measures used to assess the variables.

CASE STUDIES

These focus on one 'instance', e.g. one person who is unusual in some way. They are studied in-depth using techniques such as observations, interviews and tests. The findings may have clinical use or may be compared to 'normal' instances.

Strengths of case studies

They provide more detailed data than other methods and avoid overlooking information that could be lost by averaging. Rare situations that could not ethically or practically be produced can be investigated. When many different techniques produce the same findings validity is improved.

Weaknesses of case studies

Findings from these unique instances are unlikely to generalise and may be hard to verify, lowering reliability. Validity is reduced if the researcher loses objectivity by getting to know the individual or if their theoretical view biases their interpretation. Ethical issues are raised if the rarity of a case means that confidentiality cannot be assured.

DESIGNING INVESTIGATIONS

An **aim** can be expressed as a **hypothesis**, predicting either that there will be (a correlational) relationship or (an experimental) difference (**non-directional**) or that one experimental condition will be 'better' or a correlation will be positive or negative (**directional**). **Operationalisation** ensures that **variables** are accurately measured or manipulated by defining them clearly. This may be achieved through a **pilot study**, which checks the method to improve **validity** (to be sure the measures used are testing what they are supposed to), and **reliability** (whether the measures are consistent) and to limit potential **investigator effects**. This may also help to decide on the **sampling technique**. **Opportunity sampling** is easy as it uses readily available people but the sample is unrepresentative. **Random sampling** is more representative as everyone in the population being studied has an equal chance of being chosen, but it is harder to do and some people may be difficult to access, making it biased. **Volunteer sampling** uses requests for participants so is easy and the participants will be willing but the sample may be biased if only certain people respond.

Designing experiments

The researcher needs to **operationalise** the **independent** and **dependent variables** and choose an experimental design. They will also consider the procedure, e.g. choosing apparatus, materials and standardised instructions to control for extraneous variables and limit demand characteristics.

Designing self-reports

The researcher needs to choose whether to do a questionnaire or interview and to ensure that the questions are understandable and ethical, that closed questions offer suitable options and if not whether open questions are needed too. They may consider the use of filler questions and the ordering of Likert scales.

Designing observations

The researcher may begin with non-focused observations to select relevant and independent behavioural categories. They then operationalise them to ensure high inter-observer reliability. They also need to plan whether observers will be disclosed or not and whether they will be a participant or not.

BPS ETHICAL GUIDELINES AND HOW TO DEAL WITH THEM

Participants should give *real* consent. If not, presumptive consent could be obtained or they must be able to withdraw. Deception should be avoided. If used, participants should be told the real aim as soon as possible and allowed to take their results away. When participants know they have been in a study they should be debriefed quickly and should leave in at least as positive a mood as they started. Participants should be told they have the right to withdraw from the study at any time (regardless of payment). Their data should remain confidential unless they have agreed otherwise (e.g. not storing names with data). Their privacy should not be invaded, e.g. observations should only take place where people expect to be seen. They should be protected from physical and psychological harm, e.g. by using experienced people for risky procedures and stopping studies if unexpected risks arise.

ANALYSING QUANTITATIVE DATA: MEASURES OF CENTRAL TENDENCY AND DISPERSION

Measures of central tendency are ways to illustrate a 'typical' score. They are the **mode** (most frequent), the **median** (middle score) and the **mean** (worked out by adding up all the scores and dividing by the number of scores). **Measures of dispersion** are ways to describe how spread out the scores are. They **range** is the difference between the smallest and the largest score. The **standard deviation** calculates the average variation either side of the mean and more variation produces a larger standard deviation.

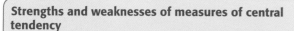

Strengths and weaknesses of measures of central tendency

The mode can be used with any data and isn't swayed by odd, very big or small scores, but isn't very informative as it ignores most of the data. The median is not affected by extreme scores either and represents a more central score. The mean takes all scores into account so is most informative, but is affected by extreme scores and should only be used with interval or ratio data.

Strengths and weaknesses of measures of dispersion

The range is easy to calculate and relates directly to actual scores, but ignores most of the scores and can be misleading if there is even one extreme score. The standard deviation is harder to calculate, but uses every score so is more informative (although the importance of odd, very large or small scores may be hidden).

TABLES AND GRAPHS

Tables are used to present raw data or summaries of data (e.g. measures of central tendency and spread). **Graphs** include bar charts, histograms and frequency distributions.

Bar charts

A bar chart is used for data in discrete categories, e.g. nominal data or measures of central tendency.

Histograms and frequency distributions

A histogram is used to illustrate continuous data with a bar for the frequency of each score. A frequency distribution illustrates the frequency of each score with a point. These are joined up to form a line.

3.13 Research Methods in Psychology Scenarios

Scenario 1: Puppy Love

Designing studies

Janusz and Caitlin are investigating children's attachment to pets that can be cuddled, like kittens and puppies, and ones that can't, like fish. They have considered using the babies that parents bring to school when they drop off older children, but they will all have an older sibling. Instead, they are putting an advert up on the local supermarket noticeboard.

Identify the following about Janusz and Caitlin's study:

- The research method is an experiment. What is the experimental design?

- What are the advantages of this design?

- What are the independent and dependent variables? Operationalise each one.

- What sampling method did they consider first?

- Why was it important that they didn't use the first sampling method they considered?

- What was the sampling method they finally decided to use?

- Write a non-directional hypothesis for Janusz and Caitlin's study.

Non-experimental methods

Caitlin's younger brother Alex has a pet rabbit. She and Janusz decide to study Alex in detail. They watch him interacting with the rabbit and record what he does. One day the rabbit bounces away and Alex laughs. Then a car backfires outside the house and Alex starts to cry. He reaches for the rabbit, but it hops away.

Answer the following questions about this aspect of Janusz and Caitlin's study:

- Which research method are they using here?

- What technique are they using to record Alex's behaviour?

- Operationalise two behavioural categories they could use to record Alex's behaviour.

- Why might Caitlin be more subjective when she is recording behaviour than Janusz?

- This could affect inter-observer reliability. Why does this matter?

- This could serve as a pilot study if they extended their study. How could it be useful?

- Janusz decides to explore the idea further with a questionnaire. Write one open and two closed questions (using different question types) that Janusz could use.

Descriptive statistics

Janusz and Caitlin need to summarise their data for the rest of their class. They have two sources of information: one is the number of children who have 'cuddly' and 'non-cuddly' pets: the other is a parental rating of how often the child cries, for children with 'cuddly' and 'non-cuddly' pets.

Answer the following questions about how Janusz and Caitlin should present their data:

(a) Which measure of central tendency should they use for the total numbers of children with 'cuddly' and 'non-cuddly' pets?

(b) Which measures of central tendency and dispersion should they use for parental ratings of crying by children with 'cuddly' and 'non-cuddly' pets?

(c) Which graph should they use to present the measure of central tendency for the ratings of crying by children with 'cuddly' and 'non-cuddly' pets?

Scenario 2: Quizzing witnesses

Correlations

Accuracy of eyewitness testimony and anxiety are related. Are anxious people better witnesses? Do anxious people end up getting involved in crimes? Are the best witnesses used more often and are they anxious because they have witnessed lots of crimes?

Use your understanding of research methods in psychology to answer these questions:

- Write a directional hypothesis relating to any aspect of the source above.

- Write a non-directional hypothesis relating to the same aspect of the source above.

- When studying eyewitness testimony demand characteristics are often a problem. What are demand characteristics?

- Investigator effects are also a problem. What are experimenter effects and are they more or less likely to be a problem when studying eyewitnesses to real crimes?

Ethics, validity and reliability

In a study of eyewitness testimony, people at a concert saw a staged episode where the guitarist in the support band was stabbed. He was carried off stage on a stretcher. At the end of the whole performance, the audience were given a questionnaire to take home.

Answer the following questions about the aims and procedure of the study:

- What was the aim of this study?

- Name **two** ethical issues raised by this study and suggest how they could be resolved.

- Studies on real eyewitnesses raise different ethical issues from lab studies. Why?

- Identify **one** strength and **one** weakness of this experiment in terms of validity.

- Would this study be likely to be more or less reliable than a lab study? Why?

- What was the sampling method and how might this have affected the results?

- Identify **one** possible extraneous variable in this study and explain why it might have been important.

Qualitative and quantitative data

The questionnaire contained questions such as:

- How did you feel when the guitarist was stabbed?
  Do you go to concerts often? *Yes / No*

- Has this event made you nervous about seeing a band in the future? *Yes / No / A little*

- Describe how aware you felt of possible threats on the way home after the concert.

Using your understanding:

(a) Identify **two** open and **two** closed questions from the list above.

(b) Which questions would collect qualitative data and which collect quantitative data?

(c) Suggest **two** themes that could be used to interpret the answers to the open questions.

Study note

The research methods section has lots of terms you need to learn. Work in a group with other students and divide the words between you. Use the glossary to make cards with the term on one side and the definition on the other. You could then use the cards to learn the terms and to test each other.

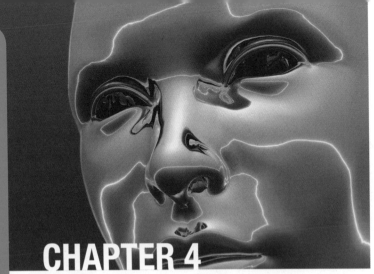

CHAPTER 4
Biological Psychology

4.1 An Introduction to Biological Psychology

YOU NEED TO:

know what these terms mean:

- biological psychology
- stress
- stress management

be able to explain:

- the sympathomedullary pathway
- the pituitary-adrenal system
- the relationship between stress and illness
- emotion- and problem-focused approaches to coping, and distinguish between them

describe and evaluate:

- how life changes and daily hassles affect stress
- the relationship between personality and stress

understand and apply your knowledge of biological psychology to:

- the problems of workplace stress
- psychological and physiological methods of stress management

KEY TERMS

biological psychology
this area focuses on explaining thinking, emotion and cognition in terms of bodily systems, e.g. the nervous system and hormones

stress   our biological and psychological responses to threats we feel we cannot overcome

stress management   the use of external strategies such as cognitive behavioural therapy, rational emotive behaviour therapy, drugs or biofeedback to reduce the impact of stressors

4.2 The Biology of Stress

Stress

The **biological approach** considers the role of bodily systems in thinking, emotions and behaviour, e.g. the role of neurotransmitters, the brain and hormones. All of these biological aspects are involved in our response to stress. **Stress** is the biological and psychological response we experience when we encounter a threat (a **stressor**) that we feel we cannot overcome by avoiding or changing the situation.

The autonomic nervous system and the adrenal medulla

In a threatening situation fast action is vital so the **sympathetic nervous system** (sANS) is activated quickly in response to stress. This is part of the **autonomic nervous system** (ANS) and causes immediate changes, e.g. releasing glucose, increasing breathing and heart rate and dilating your pupils; effects which help you to run away or defend yourself. The sANS also triggers the release of the hormone **adrenaline** from the **adrenal medulla** (an **endocrine gland**). Adrenaline has similar effects to the sANS, preparing us for 'flight or fight', but as hormones travel in the blood, these are slower and longer lasting compared to the rapid, short-lived effect of the nervous system. **Noradrenaline** is also released from the adrenal medulla into the bloodstream. It is a neurotransmitter rather than a hormone and helps to maintain sympathetic activation. This causes **positive feedback** as the more noradrenaline is released the more the sANS is activated and the more it stimulates the release of noradrenaline. To break this cycle another part of the ANS, the **parasympathetic nervous system** (pANS), returns the body to normal.

The sympathomedullary pathway

The system linking the sANS and the adrenal medulla is called the **sympathomedullary pathway** (SMP), which controls our response to acute (short-term) stressors. The SMP itself is under the control of the **hypothalamus**, a brain area which can trigger the action of the sANS and pANS and monitors hormone levels.

The pituitary gland and the adrenal cortex

In chronic (long-term) stress the release of **cortisol** (a hormone which increases blood pressure and makes energy available from the liver) is controlled by a sequence of changes. The hypothalamus releases **corticotrophin-releasing hormone** (CRH) which travels in the blood to the pituitary gland, which releases **adrenocorticotropic hormone** (ACTH). This makes the **adrenal cortex** release cortisol, but only while the stressor is present as it is controlled by a **negative feedback** loop. When the hypothalamus detects cortisol in the blood it reduces the release of CRH thus slowing cortisol release. The hypothalamus also reduces sympathetic activation so when cortisol is produced, adrenaline production reduces.

The pituitary-adrenal system

The link between the pituitary and adrenal glands is called the **pituitary-adrenal system** (PAS). The PAS controls our response to persistent threats, e.g. having a stressful job.

Revision note

Draw a flowchart showing the links between the structures (autonomic nervous system, adrenal glands, pituitary gland and hypothalamus) and what they do.

 Exam focus

Pair up each gland on the left with **one** effect on the right.　　　　*(3 marks)*

1. Adrenal cortex	a) Releases adrenaline
2. Pituitary gland	b) Releases cortisol
3. Adrenal medulla	c) Releases adrenocorticotropic hormone

Examiner commentary

The answers are: 1b, 2c, 3a. Because ACTH contains 'adreno' and 'cortico' it's easy to get it muddled with corticotrophin-releasing hormone. 'Tropic' refers to a 'directional response' so ACTH means 'going *towards* the adrenal cortex'.

4.3 Stress and Illness

Stress-related illness

Long-term stress is linked to ill health. Cortisol increases blood pressure, putting strain on the heart and increasing the risk of **cardiovascular diseases** such as coronary heart disease (CHD). The **immune system** (which fights disease) also suffers because cortisol changes how key cells (e.g. **lymphocytes**) respond, increasing the risk of disease. Cohen *et al.* (1993) found that people with more stressful lives were more likely to become infected when given the cold virus experimentally. Marucha *et al.* (1998) found that at exam times, students were slower to recover from an injury than in the holidays. **Killer T cells** (lymphocytes which remove cancerous cells) also become less effective, increasing the risk of developing cancer.

Exam focus

Table 1: The percentage of women with coronary heart disease

Number of children	Occupation	
	Housewives	*Working women*
0	No data	7
1–2	6	8
3+	5	11

The data in **Table 1** is from a study about stress and illness.
(a) Plot the data from **Table 1** on an appropriate graph. Label each axis.   *(2 marks)*
(b) Draw **two** conclusions from the data.   *(1 mark + 1 mark)*

Endel's answer:

(a)

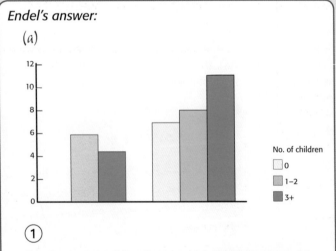

No. of children
- 0
- 1–2
- 3+

①

(b) The data show that having more children is stressful for working women, but not for housewives. The more children working women have the more stressed they get because the incidence of CHD is higher. ①+①

Revision note

When you are reading any question in an exam, remember to look at how many marks it is worth — beware of spending too long on a detailed answer for a question that is only worth 2 marks and then not having time to finish the paper.

Examiner commentary

In part (a) Endel has drawn the graph accurately, earning 1 mark, but needed 'Percentage coronary heart disease' on the y-axis, 'Occupation' (housewives/working women) on the x-axis and a graph title to earn the second mark. His part (b) answer is detailed and accurate.

Thinking psychologically

The study in the question above found that working women were, overall, more likely to have CHD than housewives, especially if they had little social support at work (Haynes *et al.*, 1980). How do these findings relate to the idea that stress is linked to ill health?

4.4 Stress and Everyday Life: life changes and daily hassles

Stress and life events

It makes sense that a major crisis, such as someone dying, would be stressful. However, Holmes & Rahe (1967) suggested that any **life changes**, even good ones, are stressful as they require readjustment so can affect our health. Using a questionnaire to identify 43 major life events, each having a value for 'Life Change Units' according to how traumatic it felt, they produced the **social readjustment rating scale** (SRRS). This gives a mean 'stress score' to each event (e.g. *Death of spouse* = 100, *Marriage* = 50, *Pregnancy* = 40, *Vacation* = 13, *Christmas* = 12). A high total score, e.g. for the last six months, indicates the individual has experienced more stress.

Stressful life events and ill health

Life events are related to ill health – a higher SRRS score is linked to a greater risk of illness. Rahe *et al.* (1970) found that for crew members on-board a ship, the higher their SRRS scores for the six months before departure, the more likely they were to be ill over the following six to eight months. Yamada *et al.* (2003) found that higher SRRS scores were associated with a greater risk of developing a disease in which organs develop lumps, and Palesh *et al.* (2007) found that women who had had breast cancer were more likely to relapse if they had higher SRRS scores.

Not all evidence shows a link between life events and ill health. Vidal *et al.* (2006) followed up patients with inflammatory bowel disease (IBD) who were in remission (i.e. had no current symptoms). Over 11 months there was no relationship between relapse of IBD and stressful life events.

Life events and coping with stressors

Stressful life events also seem to make us more vulnerable to other stressors. Bonanno *et al.* (2007) studied the effects of the attacks on the World Trade Centre in 2001 on people living close by. People with fewer recent life events before the disaster coped better. Those with only one recent life event were about twice as likely to be resilient to the effects as those who had experienced two or three, suggesting that the effects of stressful life events are cumulative.

Exam focus

The graph on the right illustrates the data from a study about stress.

(a) Name the type of graph shown. *(1 mark)*
(b) (i) What type of relationship is shown on the graph? *(2 marks)*
    (ii) Explain what the relationship shown on the graph tells us about stress. *(2 marks)*

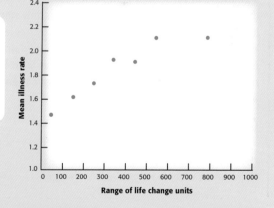

Charlie's answer:

(a) It's a line graph because the dots fall in a line showing a positive correlation. **(0)**

(b) (i) It's a positive correlation. **(2)**

    (ii) It shows that being more stressed causes you to get ill. **(0)**

Examiner commentary
(a) Although the points do fall in an approximate line, this doesn't make it a line graph – it's a scattergram. (b) (i) This is correct – one mark for saying it's a correlation, the other for identifying it as a positive correlation. In (b) (ii) Charlie has made a common mistake; we cannot draw conclusions about causality from single correlations. He could have earned one mark for saying there was a link or relationship between stress (the number of life change units) and illness, or two for saying that higher stress levels were related to a higher incidence of illness.

Daily hassles

It isn't only the big things in life that cause stress. According to Lazarus, day-to-day problems cause us stress. The **Hassles Scale** (Kanner *et al.*, 1981) includes 117 events that could annoy people on a daily basis, e.g. queuing or having an argument. People who had the most hassles suffered more psychological symptoms of stress, such as depression and anxiety. Kanner *et al.* also developed the **Uplifts Scale**, which measures 135 good things, e.g. getting enough sleep or eating out. Uplifts alone do not seem to relate to health but together with hassles they affect how we view a situation: if it is more negative it will be more damaging to us, so having uplifts helps us to cope.

Hassles and ill health

DeLongis *et al.* (1988) found that people with more stressors were more likely to get flu, headaches and backache. As the scale measured their *perception* of stress it showed that this was more important than the volume of stressors they were exposed to, which matters because stress is caused by feeling that one cannot cope with a threat.

Newman *et al.* (2007) investigated a link between the biology of stress, daily hassles and unhealthy behaviour. They found that in women whose cortisol levels were highly reactive to stressful situations, hassles and snacking were linked: when they had more hassles they ate more snacks. This didn't happen in women with less reactive cortisol levels. Courtois *et al.* (2007) found that both life events and daily hassles affected adolescent alcohol and tobacco use, although the link to daily hassles was stronger. Adolescents with more hassles started drinking and smoking earlier and became more dependent.

Daily hassles and coping with stressors

Waldrop *et al.* (2007) found that people with lots of current hassles find it harder to deal with previous stressors, such as childhood abuse. This, and the effect of daily hassles on behaviours such as poor eating and drug use, suggests that hassles make coping with stressors more difficult and makes it even more likely that health may be affected.

Exam focus

Peter has a new job, a house and his parents nearby to lend a hand. However, he finds the gardening a nuisance, hates painting the house, thinks he can't get a girlfriend because he's going bald and is forever losing things. Steph also has a good job but she only started it recently, having been made redundant by her last employer. That was just after her dad had died and she'd moved out of her house and back in to live with her mum. They went on holiday together to give themselves a break.

(a) Use an example from the text above to explain what is meant by 'daily hassles'. *(3 marks)*

(b) Use an example from the text above to explain what is meant by 'life changes'. *(3 marks)*

Jade's answer:

(a) Daily hassles are things like worrying about what you look like — like Peter thinking he's going bald. Although they are quite minor they add up to make us stressed. They can, however, be countered by some good things, called uplifts, like if Peter spends time with his mum and dad or likes the house when he's painted it. The more hassles you have, especially if you have few uplifts, means you are more likely to feel stressed and get ill. ②

(b) Life changes are the big bad things, like going to prison. These are much more serious than hassles and are also linked to health. The more life change units you have in a short space of time the more likely you are to get ill. ①

Examiner commentary

Jade's answer to part (a) is quite basic. She has given an example (earning one mark) and hinted that daily hassles are the little irritations that happen often, but has not clearly explained what they are, so only earns one of the two marks for explaining. The part on uplifts is irrelevant to this question. In her answer to (b) Jade's explanation is very basic as it lacks both clarity and accuracy, for example, omitting the idea that even readjustment to good things can cause stress. She cannot earn a mark for the example as the one she gives is not from the text.

4.5 Stress and Personality

The Type A personality

Rosenman & Friedman (1958) found a link between stress and illness. They described the **Type A personality** as people who are competitive, aggressive and goal-directed, but also have high stress levels and are more likely to develop coronary heart disease (CHD). People with the more laid-back **Type B personality**, or Type X which isn't clearly in either category, suffer less CHD.

Type A: more easily stressed or more stress-seeking?

Forgays *et al.* (2001) compared stress in at-home and working mums. Regardless of occupation, the Type A personalities found motherhood more stressful. This suggests that Type A individuals find situations more stressful than other people. However, Perry & Baldwin (2000) found that Type A personality was linked to aggressive driving behaviour. This could be because Type As are more likely to drive aggressively, i.e. their personality causes them to behave in ways that increase exposure to stress.

Health and personality type

Lee & Watanuki (2007) tested how stressful images affected the heartbeat and blood pressure of Type A and Type B personalities. They found that the Type A participants had a greater level of sympathetic nervous system activity controlling the heart rate than Type Bs both during rest and when under stress, and their hearts pumped more blood per minute than people with a Type B personality. In all participants, parasympathetic activity reduced the heart rate but the decrease was smaller in Type As.

Mitaishvili & Danelia (2006) found no relationship between a Type A personality and the rate of coronary heart disease. Instead they found that factors such as high job strain were associated with increased risk of CHD.

Individuals with **Type C personalities** repress their emotions, have little social support and tend to feel hopeless and helpless so get more stressed. Shaffer *et al.* (1987) found that Type C doctors were more likely to suffer from cancer. The **Type D personality** is anxious, distressed and pessimistic. Denollet (1998) found that in a sample of CHD patients, some also had cancer; although Type D wasn't the most common personality for CHD patients, these individuals were more likely to have cancer as well and were more likely to die from it. These findings show that Type A isn't the only personality linked to stress and ill health.

Exam focus

(a) Describe a personality type that is linked to stress and ill health. *(3 marks)*

(b) Using the personality type you have described in part (a) describe evidence to illustrate how it is linked to stress and ill health. *(4 marks)*

Gemma's answer:

(a) A type A personality is determined and tends to enjoy competitive sports and have high-powered jobs and rush everywhere. This behaviour might be the cause of their stress — as it puts them in demanding situations — or it could be that they are more reactive to potentially threatening situations than, say, type Bs who are more laid-back. Either way, they are more likely to be ill than type B or X, e.g. they are more likely to get heart disease. (3)

(b) A type C personality who hides everything away and bottles up their problems was shown by Shaffer et al. to be more likely to get ill because type C doctors got cancer more than other personalities. Denollet also found personality was linked to cancer. Type D patients with heart disease were more likely to get cancer too and more likely to die than other personalities. (0)

Examiner commentary

Gemma's description in (a) is sufficient for three marks. Her answer to (b) is also detailed, but parts (a) and (b) of the question should be linked. Gemma, however, has focused on different aspects of personality in parts (a) and (b) so scores 0 for (b). In a parted question where the parts are linked you *must* make sure that your responses are linked too, otherwise only your answer to the first part will count.

4.6 Workplace Stress

Work stress and health

Being fired from work or changing jobs voluntarily are stressful life events, and daily hassles, such as losing things, can relate to work. However, some specific aspects of a job make it more or less stressful: these are sources of **work stress**. Marmot *et al.* (1997) reported that senior employees were less stressed and less likely to die from heart disease than junior ones. Although having a high workload may be stressful, being in charge – and having some control over your work – helps to limit stress. Sparks *et al.* (1997) found that people working longer hours were less healthy and Kageyama *et al.* (1998) found greater sympathetic nervous system activity (indicating greater stress levels) in people working long hours or who had a long journey to work.

Work stress and personality

Jepson & Forrest (2006) investigated stress in teachers and found that Type A behaviour was linked to perceived stress. Hallberg *et al.* (2007) found a similar pattern in nurses. 'Burnout', where an employee works so hard that they become physically and emotionally exhausted, was positively correlated with Type A behaviour. This may be because Type As strive hard to achieve and become more impatient and irritable. This negative mood seems to make them more stressed at work.

Overwork and underwork

Too much work is stressful, but 'underwork' – having too little to do or feeling your skills are underused – also leads to low job satisfaction and therefore stress. Having no job is also stressful. Hammarstrom & Janlert (1997) found that unemployment in school leavers was linked to greater signs of stress, such as anxiety and depression.

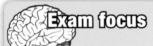 **Exam focus**

Tick **either** true **or** false for each statement. *(3 marks)*

1. An employee suddenly told they are being made redundant will release adrenaline.	True ☐ False ☐
2. A production line worker who constantly struggles to keep up will release cortisol.	True ☐ False ☐
3. A boss relaxing in their office will have an active parasympathetic nervous system.	True ☐ False ☐

Examiner commentary
All the answers are true.

Exam focus

Many factors have been found to contribute to work stress.

(a) Outline **one** factor that contributes to work stress. *(2 marks)*

(b) Suggest **another** factor that contributes to work stress that is different from the one you have outlined in part (*a*) and use research evidence to explain which factor is most important. *(4 marks)*

Mike's answer:

(a) Being underworked can be stressful. This might be having too little to do, like a person stuck at reception to meet people and answer the phone but if it isn't busy they will get bored. It can mean your job's too easy, so a shop junior left to shelf stack when they could be doing the ordering might feel they have unused skills. ②

(b) The type of person you are matters more. Type A personalities might choose really taxing jobs for the extra pressure so do well but might also find they get more stressed. Jepson & Forrest found type A teachers saw their jobs as more stressful than ones with other personality types. Also, because they are 'fast and furious' they are likely to find stuff to do and not get bored, but type As also burnout more – as Hallberg et al. found with nurses. This might be because they get more frustrated so get more stressed. ④

Examiner commentary
Mike has answered accurately and elaborated effectively with examples. He has correctly used a different factor in part (b) and has avoided the common mistake of unnecessarily describing the second factor, which is not required.

4.7 Emotion- and Problem-focused Coping

Emotion-focused coping

One way to manage a stressor is to make yourself feel better about the situation. This is called **emotion-focused** (EF) **coping**, which aims to reduce the negative effects of the stressor. Some EF strategies include taking your mind off your fear by keeping busy or eating, letting off steam to other people, praying for strength and ignoring the problem in the hope that it will go away.

Problem-focused coping

Alternatively, you can try to cope by doing something about the issue itself, this is called **problem-focused** (PF) **coping**. These strategies aim to remove or limit the cause of the stressor and include getting advice from friends or professionals, investigating alternative plans of action, doing something positive to prevent or reduce the stressor and using past experience to overcome the issue.

Emotion- versus problem-focused coping

Often we use both EF and PF strategies. Problem-focused coping is generally more effective as it removes the stressor, and it also seems to be healthier. Epping-Jordan *et al.* (1994) found that cancer patients who used EF coping, e.g. denying they were very ill, deteriorated more quickly than those who faced their problem. The effect is also quite general. Genco *et al.* (1999) found that dental patients who coped with financial problems using PF strategies had fewer problems with their teeth than those using EF coping.

However, PF coping isn't always helpful, e.g. when the individual cannot remove the source of stress; the feelings of loss associated with bereavement, for example, require EF coping. Aldridge & Roesch (2007) found that children with cancer (who could do nothing practical to help themselves) were more stressed if they tried to use PF coping. Similarly, after an industrial accident an individual can do little to reduce the problem but still needs to manage their fears in order to cope. Collins *et al.* (1983) studied how people coped with the threats posed by the meltdown at the Three Mile Island nuclear power plant in 1979. Those using EF strategies coped better than those using PF strategies (who were trying to take direct action).

Emotion-focused coping is effective in reducing real-life and experimentally induced stress. Lee *et al.* (2006) showed that a biological stress marker found in saliva increased in children when they had a blood test but that this could be prevented if they were distracted with a kaleidoscope. Toda *et al.* (2006) found that staying at a spa helped to reduce stress in women following stressful life events. Toda *et al.* (2007) experimentally tested the effect of EF distraction on subjective stress. They found that reported stress decreased after watching comic films, suggesting that laughter relieves stress by producing positive feelings.

Exam focus

Karen is stressed over her homework; some she hasn't finished and she can't do one piece at all.

(a) Describe what is meant by emotion-focused coping and suggest **two** ways that Karen could use emotion-focused coping. *(2 marks + 2 marks)*

(b) Describe what is meant by problem-focused coping and suggest **two** ways that Karen could use problem-focused coping. *(2 marks + 2 marks)*

Phil's answer:

(a) Emotion–focused coping is where you make yourself feel better, so she could give up on the homework and go to the park instead. ①+①

(b) Problem–focused coping gets rid of the stressor, like getting help from her teacher. ①+①

Examiner commentary

Phil has given basic descriptions and only one example in answer to each part question rather than two.

4.8 Psychological Stress Management Strategies

Psychological therapy: the cognitive approach

Stress management uses external influences to reduce the impact of stressors. The cognitive approach suggests that faulty thinking causes our inability to cope, so cognitive therapy aims to change our cognitions so that we can deal with the stressor. Negative and dysfunctional beliefs are challenged and behavioural tasks are used to help us to overcome our irrational thinking. This is therefore called cognitive *behavioural* therapy.

Rational emotive behaviour therapy (REBT)

Ellis (1977) suggested that activating events (A), i.e. stressors, trigger beliefs (B) about our ability to cope. If these beliefs are negative, i.e. that we cannot cope, the consequence (C) will also be negative – we will feel stressed (this is called the **ABC model**). According to Ellis, if we could control our beliefs we would be able to control our emotions and reduce the negative effects of stress. This is the aim of **rational emotive behaviour therapy** (REBT). The ABC model is extended to include the two stages of REBT: disrupting irrational beliefs (D) and the effects of this disruption (E) – which may be *cognitive* (changing irrational beliefs to rational ones), *emotional* (changing feelings from negative to positive) or *behavioural* (changing behaviour to improve coping). This enables us to withstand stressors, e.g. by rejecting the belief that a situation is intolerable or avoiding overreacting to minor problems.

A crashed the car → B cannot cope with driving → C never drive again

Does REBT work?

Balevre (2001) found that perfectionist nurses with unrealistic expectations were likely to experience burnout. REBT would have helped to make their expectations more realistic. Engels *et al.* (1993) showed that REBT was more successful in treating anxiety than behavioural therapy alone or combined with REBT. However, REBT benefits are short-term and its aggressive, challenging style raises ethical issues, especially in the face of stress. REBT also implies the problem lies within the individual when the blame may really lie elsewhere, so REBT has the potential to be abused (also see page 103).

Cognitive behavioural therapy

Beck (1976) suggested that our emotional response to a stressor depends on our cognitive processing. As cognition differs, so does ability to cope with stress. People with dysfunctional beliefs have negative automatic thoughts, such as feelings of hopelessness and self-doubt. This relationship between thoughts is circular: negative thinking generates more negative thinking. Beck illustrated this in his **cognitive triad** (see page 102). This leads the individual to identifying things as stressors when they are not.

    Cognitive behavioural therapy (CBT) aims to reduce the symptoms of emotional disorders by changing dysfunctional cognition. The therapist teaches the client to identify and monitor the negative automatic thoughts and to recognise positive events. These counter the individual's negative beliefs, demonstrating their irrationality. A stressed client may be set 'homework' to find examples of where they have dealt with a difficult situation in the past to challenge their belief that they never cope.

Does CBT work?

Pérez *et al.* (1999) found that depressed people who were put into a sad mood (using sad music and recall of unhappy memories) paid more attention to the unhappy than happy stimuli, supporting the idea that attention is biased in favour of negative cognitions. In a meta-analysis, Butler & Beck (2000) found that CBT was useful for anxious and depressed clients. The relapse rate for depression was only 29.5 per cent after CBT compared to 60 per cent with antidepressant treatment.

4.9 Physiological Stress Management Strategies

Drugs

Stress can lead to anxiety and depression, which can be treated with **drugs**. Neurons in our nervous system communicate across the gaps between them, called **synapses**, using **neurotransmitters**. Drugs can act here, affecting emotions, cognitions and behaviour, so alter the symptoms of stress. They can *mimic neurotransmitters* (have the same effect), *block receptors* (prevent their activity) or *prevent the recycling of neurotransmitters* (causing an increase in neurotransmitter level in the synapse).

Do drugs work?

In depression the levels of **serotonin** (a neurotransmitter) are lower than normal. **Selective serotonin reuptake inhibitors** (SSRIs) counteract this. These drugs prevent the recycling of serotonin and so it remains in the synapse and reduces the symptoms of depression. Trivedi *et al.* (2006) found that an SSRI (citalopram) halved the depression score of 47 per cent of patients although this depended on the person. It was most effective for well-educated, employed, white Caucasian women who were not suffering from other psychological or physical disorders. Drugs can only treat the symptoms of stress, not the cause, but being able to cope using medication in the short-term might enable someone to overcome a stressful situation in a way that would not be possible if they were feeling very anxious or depressed.

Biofeedback

In **biofeedback** the client receives ongoing data about their body functions, e.g. pulse rate, blood pressure or muscle tension. This information indicates tension or relaxation so can help the client to learn to become more relaxed. Initially, the client cannot deliberately change their state but the feedback helps them to become aware of the way their thinking and behaviour affects their biological functioning. A stressed person may discover that picturing themselves on a beach causes their blood pressure to fall, although they may not be conscious of how the change occurs.

Does biofeedback work?

Budzynski *et al.* (1973) found that patients with tension headaches could learn to reduce muscle tension (and relieve their symptoms) using feedback and that this was more effective than random feedback or attention from the experimenters. Tsai *et al.* (2007) found that biofeedback about changes in blood pressure produced a greater reduction in blood pressure in patients with high blood pressure than those given sham feedback. Nakao *et al.* (1997) found that people taught to control their blood pressure using biofeedback were able to reduce it even in a deliberately stressful laboratory situation.

Exam focus

Jenny believes that when stressors are external, such as a nasty neighbour, there is nothing we can do but wait for them to go away. Alice disagrees, arguing that there are many ways that we can reduce the effects of a stressor.

Use research evidence to support **either** Jenny **or** Alice's viewpoint.   *(6 marks)*

Irda's answer:

Stress happens. We are going to worry about it anyway but that won't help so we just need to get on with life. And even if we do go for help it doesn't always work so we might as well not have bothered and avoided getting more wound up. ②

Examiner commentary

Irda's answer gives very basic support for Alice's viewpoint (whose name should have been stated). She makes implicit references to research about the ineffectiveness of emotion-focused coping and about therapies not always working, but she needed evidence to support these ideas. Arguing in favour of Alice's viewpoint would have been easier by providing evidence that biological responses might help (e.g. to make you feel more 'brave') so that you can use problem-focused coping behaviours (such as talking to the neighbour) that are more effective, or having CBT to overcome fears about doing so. Research supporting any of these ideas (e.g. Epping-Jordan *et al.* or Butler & Beck) could have earned marks.

4.10 Summary

STRESS

Stress is a biological and psychological response to a threatening **stressor**. The **biological approach** explains the response to stress in terms of neurotransmitters, the brain and hormones.

The SMP

The **sympathomedullary pathway** responds quickly to an acute stressor. The sympathetic part of the autonomic nervous system provides extra energy and oxygen so we can run or fight. It also triggers **adrenaline** release, which has similar effects but these are slower and last longer. **Noradrenaline** is also released, which maintains sympathetic activation through positive feedback.

The PAS

The **pituitary-adrenal system** provides a long-term response to chronic stressors. Production of corticotrophin-releasing hormone (CRH) from the hypothalamus is controlled by negative feedback so persists only while the stressor is present. CRH triggers the release of adrenocorticotropic hormone from the pituitary gland and therefore the release of **cortisol** from the adrenal cortex. This hormone replaces the effect of adrenaline.

STRESS AND HEALTH

Cortisol increases blood pressure and increases the risk of cardiovascular disease. The **immune system** becomes less effective, increasing the risk of diseases and cancer, e.g. Cohen *et al.* found that stress made people susceptible to colds and Marucha *et al.* found that when stressed, students recovered more slowly from injuries.

Life events

Holmes & Rahe suggested that **life changes**, good or bad, are stressful because we have to readjust. People with higher scores on the **Social Readjustment Rating Scale** are at greater risk of illness. Rahe *et al.* found that sailors with high SRRS scores were more likely to get ill and Palesh *et al.* found higher relapse rates of breast cancer in women with higher SRRS scores. However, life events do not always lead to worse health. Vidal *et al.* found no relationship between relapse of bowel disease and stressful life events.

Hassles and health

The **Hassles Scale** measures the daily problems that cause us stress, e.g. having too much to do or getting interrupted. If we see hassles as a problem we suffer because we feel unable to cope – this is stressful. Having more hassles is related to greater symptoms of stress, e.g. depression and anxiety, although having **uplifts** as well (e.g. getting on well with your friends or partner) reduces the impact of hassles on health by helping us to cope.

DeLongis *et al.* found that people with more hassles were more likely to get flu, headaches and backache. Courtois *et al.* found that daily hassles were more closely linked to adolescent drinking and smoking than life events.

Life events and coping

Bonanno *et al.* found that people with fewer life events before a disaster cope better. This suggests that the effects of stressful life events build up, making us less resilient to stress.

Daily hassles and coping

Waldrop *et al.* found that having many hassles made it harder to cope with previous stressors, e.g. childhood abuse. As daily hassles also increase unhealthy behaviours like poor eating and drug use, they seem to make coping with stressors harder.

STRESS AND PERSONALITY

Rosenman & Friedman (1958) suggested that people with **Type A personalities** were impatient, competitive and hostile. Such individuals had high stress levels and were at higher risk from heart disease than Type B or Type X people.

Type A: stressy or stress-seeking?

Forgays *et al.* found that regardless of whether Type A mothers were at-home or working, they found motherhood more stressful than mums with other personality types, suggesting that Type A individuals find situations more stressful. Perry & Baldwin, however, showed that the Type A personality was linked to aggressive driving. This suggests the behaviour of Type As gets them into situations that increase stress.

Health and personality

Lee & Watanuki found that Type As' hearts worked harder and responded more to stressful situations that those of Type Bs, suggesting that the link to health may be a physiological rather than psychological one. However, Mitaishvili & Danelia found no link between Type A and heart disease, but identified factors like job strain as increasing risk.

Other personalities are also associated with stress and poor health. **Type Cs** (with repressed emotions and little social support) get more stressed. Shaffer *et al.* found Type Cs were more likely to develop cancer. **Type Ds** are anxious and pessimistic. Denollet found that Type D heart disease patients were more likely to also develop cancer than other personality types.

WORK STRESS AND HEALTH

Aspects of the social and physical environment where we are employed can cause **work stress** and this can affect health, e.g. managers might have hassles from job pressures. Having a long journey to work and long working hours are linked to higher stress levels (Kageyama *et al.*) and long hours are also linked to ill health (Sparks *et al.*). Marmot *et al.* reported that lower-grade workers were more likely to be stressed and to die from heart disease than higher-grade ones. This may be because having control over your work demands (e.g. when more senior) can limit stress.

Work stress and personality

Type A teachers (Jepson & Forrest) and nurses (Hallberg *et al.*) experience more stress. This may be because they strive hard, so get impatient and irritable and this is stressful.

Over- and underwork

Having too much work can be a daily hassle or a chronic stressor. Underwork, either having too little to do or feeling underused, is also stressful as is not having a job.

EMOTION-FOCUSED COPING

Emotion-focused (EF) **coping** aims to reduce negative effects, e.g. distress, making us feel better without removing the source of stress, e.g. denial or crying.

PROBLEM-FOCUSED COPING

Problem-focused (PF) **coping** aims to reduce stress by removing the stressor, e.g. getting advice or taking control.

Emotion- versus problem-focused coping

By alleviating the cause rather than just the consequence, PF coping is generally more effective – and healthier – than EF coping, e.g. cancer patients using EF coping deteriorate faster than those using PF (Epping-Jordan *et al.*). However, if the stressor cannot be removed, e.g. when someone dies, EF coping is more effective than PF. Aldridge & Roesch found that as child cancer patients could do nothing practical to solve their problem they were more stressed if they tried to use PF coping. Following an industrial accident, people using EF strategies – and managing their fears – coped better than those using PF strategies (Collins *et al.*) as there was little direct action they could do take change what had already happened.

Experimental evidence supports the use of EF coping. Lee *et al.* found that children having blood tests were less stressed when distracted (an EF strategy) with a kaleidoscope and Toda *et al.* found that funny films (another EF strategy) made people feel less stressed.

PSYCHOLOGICAL STRESS MANAGEMENT STRATEGIES

The cognitive approach to psychological **stress management** aims to change our cognitions so we can deal with stressors. The techniques include **rational emotive behaviour therapy** (REBT) and **cognitive behavioural therapy** (CBT).

REBT

According to Ellis, stressors (activating events, A) trigger beliefs (B) about being unable to cope and, as a consequence (C), we feel stressed. REBT aims to enable us to control our beliefs and therefore control our emotions, reducing the negative effects of stress. Disrupting irrational beliefs (D) has effects (E) such as making irrational beliefs into rational ones, changing negative feelings to positive ones and changing our behaviour so we cope better.

CBT

According to Beck, dysfunctional beliefs, e.g. about failing to cope with stress, create more negative thinking as illustrated in the cognitive triad, so make coping harder. CBT aims to change dysfunctional cognition by identifying negative automatic thoughts and helping the client to recognise positive events.

REBT in practice

Balevre found that nurses with unrealistic expectations were more likely to burnout, suggesting that beliefs do have consequences for stress, and Engels *et al.* found that REBT worked better for anxious patients than behavioural or combined therapy. However, the benefits of REBT are short-term and its challenging style is ethically questionable as is the implication that stress is the individual's problem.

CBT in practice

Pérez *et al.* found that depressed people paid more attention to the unhappy than happy stimuli, showing that they were biased towards negative thinking. Butler & Beck found that CBT helped anxious and depressed clients. Twice as many people relapsed into depression after antidepressant treatment than after CBT.

PHYSIOLOGICAL STRESS MANAGEMENT STRATEGIES

Symptoms of stress can be treated with **drugs** which mimic, block or enhance the action of neurotransmitters. In **biofeedback**, data about tension in the patient's body enable them to learn to become aware of factors such as pulse rate and blood pressure and to relax.

Drugs

Selective serotonin reuptake inhibitors (SSRIs) are used to treat the symptoms of depression by raising the level of serotonin. Trivedi *et al.* found that an SSRI halved the depression score of patients. This effect, however, was better for some people than others. Drugs only treat the symptoms of stress, not the cause, but short-term coping can ease a stressful situation enabling the person to overcome the source of stress.

Biofeedback

Budzynski *et al.* found that biofeedback reduced symptoms in patients with headaches as they learned to reduce muscle tension. Tsai *et al.* found that patients with high blood pressure learned to reduce it using biofeedback, and Nakao *et al.* showed that biofeedback could be used to reduce blood pressure even in stressful situations.

4.11 Biological Psychology Scenarios

Scenario 1: Jamie and the giant perch

Long-term loser

Jamie is the champion fisherman in his club – he caught a giant perch last year – and is under pressure to defend his title. However, he has had a run of bad luck leading up to the final competition. First he had his fishing tackle stolen when his house was broken into, then he found he'd accidentally let his Angler's Club membership expire when he moved house; he was told it was too late to re-register, so he spent two weeks trying to sort it out, and couldn't even go to the river without his permit. As he wasn't out fishing each evening he was pestered into doing jobs like gardening and DIY. While he was painting the ceiling, he fell off the ladder, smashed the glass case containing the giant perch and broke his leg.

Using your understanding of factors affecting stress, identify possible life events and daily hassles that Jamie might find stressful. Explain how life events and daily hassles can affect us.

The stressors Jamie has been experiencing have been going on for some time. Using your understanding of the biology of stress, explain how Jamie's body is likely to have responded to these long-term problems.

Short-term shakes

By the day of the competition, Jamie has recovered from the broken bone and has renewed his membership, but he is much more nervous than he expected. In the morning he is too anxious to eat breakfast and when someone slaps him on the back to wish him luck, he jumps sky-high. He starts to unpack his stuff beside the water but finds his hands are shaking too much to do it.

Using your understanding of the biology of stress, explain how Jamie's body is responding to the short-term threat of the competition.

The pressure of personality

When Jamie broke his leg it was the first time he'd ever been to hospital. In fact, Jamie hadn't been to see his doctor in years – unlike his brother Fred who always seemed to be ill; even though he was only in his early 40s he had high blood pressure. He was also the opposite of Jamie in terms of personality; while Jamie was generally calm and relaxed about life, Fred was constantly on the go. He would run everywhere and could never sit still. Fred had a fast car and, although like Jamie he enjoyed the water, Fred preferred to water-ski than just sit and fish.

Using the example of Jamie and Fred, explain how personality can affect stress and health.

Scenario 2: Carolyn's crisis

Working and what works: strategies for stress

Carolyn can't settle into her first job. She left university last year with a good degree but has always felt a bit of a failure. She thinks her father was disappointed that she didn't go to the same university as he did and she hasn't kept in contact with the people she knew on her course because she was sure they only hung around with her so she would help them with their coursework, not because they actually liked her. Some of them have sent her emails and texts inviting her to stay but she hasn't replied as she isn't sure they really mean it. The more Carolyn tries to cope at work, the harder it gets. Nobody seems to want to talk to her and she finds the work difficult even though she knows it shouldn't be. Sometimes she gets so upset she finds her heart thumping in her chest and simply wants to rush out of the building. Two managers tell her how things should be done but their instructions are totally different so she doesn't know which to follow. She often ends up missing lunch or staying late to get everything done. They even tell her how she should do simple things like set up basic documents and spreadsheets, which is frustrating because they are a bit clueless: she could do it much better if they just left her alone.

Using your understanding of work stress, explain **one or more** reasons why Carolyn might be finding her new job difficult to cope with.

Carolyn's work problems are making her so stressed that she is losing sleep and getting really upset. Explain how **either** a psychological **or** a biological stress management strategy could help her. Justify your choice and explain what the therapy would involve in Carolyn's case and why.

Is Carolyn coping?

When Carolyn gets home from work she gives herself a treat, like a big bar of chocolate, or goes for a walk in the park to distract her from the problems she's had during the day. At first she used to phone her sister, Jade, but talking simply made her cry so now she just keeps her feelings to herself.

Using your understanding of coping strategies, decide whether Carolyn is using predominantly emotion- or problem-focused strategies.

Explain the difference between emotion- and problem-focused strategies and use evidence to show why the strategies Carolyn is using are sometimes useful.

Describe what Carolyn might do if she were to use the alternative coping strategy and use evidence to show why this might be more useful.

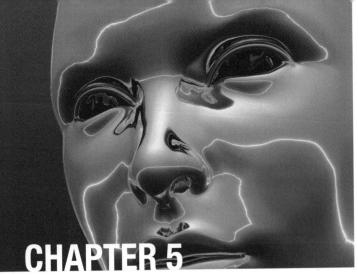

CHAPTER 5
Social Psychology

5.1 An Introduction to Social Psychology: social influence

YOU NEED TO:

know what these terms mean:

- conformity
- internalisation
- compliance
- obedience

describe and evaluate:

- informational social influence as an explanation of conformity
- normative social influence as an explanation of conformity
- Milgram's research into obedience
- explanations of obedience

be able to explain:

- independent behaviour including resisting pressure to conform and to obey
- individual differences in independent behaviour including locus of control

understand and apply your knowledge of social influence, including:

- the implications for social change of research into social influence

KEY TERMS

conformity a type of majority influence which occurs when a larger group of people influences a smaller number and individuals in the smaller group adjust their behaviour or opinions to fit in with the majority

internalisation changing our private attitudes and public behaviour to mirror those of a group

compliance changing our behaviour to go along with the majority without agreeing with them, or changing our minds about how we would like to act

obedience following direct orders from a person in a position of authority over us

5.2 Conformity

Conformity

Conformity is a type of majority influence that occurs when the behaviour or opinions of a smaller group of people (the minority) change to fit in with a bigger group (the majority). If this influence occurs because the majority have convinced us they are correct then we **internalise** their beliefs and our behaviour will change. Alternatively, we may change our beliefs or behaviours to match those of the majority because we admire them and want to be like them, i.e. we **identify** with them. If we do not actually change our minds, but alter our behaviour to fit in with the majority, then we are **complying**.

The Asch demonstration of compliance

Asch (1955) told the participants they were involved in a study about vision. Each participant sat with several confederates around a table or in a line. Each person named line A, B or C (see Figure 5.1) as matching the length of the target line X, with the real participant judging last (or last but one). At first, the confederates gave the correct answer, but when they all gave the wrong answer the real participants conformed in nearly 37 per cent of the critical trials. Control participants answered correctly in all but three of 720 trials (less than 1 per cent errors). When interviewed, many of Asch's participants said that they knew their answers were wrong so they had not internalised the group answer but just complied with their response, although some genuinely believed that the majority opinion was true, thinking they had eye strain or their chairs were in such a position that they couldn't see the cards properly.

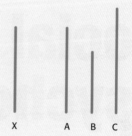

Figure 5.1 Lines like those used by Asch (1955).

Compliance versus internalisation

In Asch's study internalisation was unlikely as most participants didn't believe the confederates' responses. Holzhausen & McGlynn (2001) investigated a situation with less certainty. Participants were asked publicly (to test compliance) and privately (to test internalisation) whether they agreed with answers to maths problems they were told were the majority view. If the problems were easy and the answers credible most participants both complied and internalised the response, but if the answers seemed implausible, they complied without internalising. However, when the problems were difficult, they both internalised and complied regardless of the credibility of the answer suggesting that when the correct response to a situation is unclear we tend to internalise the norms of our group.

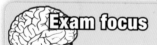 Exam focus

Exam focus

Pair up each term on the left with **one** statement on the right.

(3 marks)

1. Internalisation	a) Changing our actions to match the majority without altering our beliefs.
2. Conformity	b) Changing our beliefs and consequently our behaviour because the majority have persuaded us that the view they hold is right.
3. Compliance	c) The influence of a majority group on a minority group that causes the beliefs and/or behaviour of the minority to change to match the majority.

Examiner commentary

The answers are: 1b, 2c, 3a. Note that 'conformity' is a general concept whereas compliance and internalisation specify whether *beliefs* change as well as behaviour.

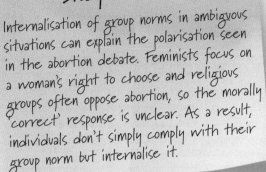

Study note

One important application of findings on conformity is to jury decision making. Even if a juror disagrees with the initial majority vote (of innocence or guilt) by the jury, it is highly likely that they will agree by the end and conformity can help to explain why.

Study note

Internalisation of group norms in ambiguous situations can explain the polarisation seen in the abortion debate. Feminists focus on a woman's right to choose and religious groups often oppose abortion, so the morally 'correct' response is unclear. As a result, individuals don't simply comply with their group norm but internalise it.

Normative social influence

Normative influence occurs when we conform to majority behaviour, e.g. in order to be liked or accepted or to avoid rejection, without changing what we believe. This can explain the conformity in Asch's study – in a new social situation the participants felt anxious and wanted to be accepted by the group so changed their public behaviour even though their private beliefs stayed the same. Griskevicius *et al.* (2006) investigated how conformity might act to reduce rejection (e.g. threats) or increase acceptance (e.g. attract mates). Students either read a story about a house break-in (to prime self-protection) or a holiday love affair (to prime mate attraction). They then logged into a chat room in groups of four and judged paintings. After self-protection priming both genders conformed more to their group's opinion of the paintings than controls. In the mate-attraction condition women conformed more than controls, but men conformed less. This shows that the need for self-protection leads to conformity in men and women. However, the desire for a mate affects the sexes differently, making women more conformist and men less so.

Normative influence in real life

Verkooijen *et al.* (2007) found that membership of youth subcultures was related to drug use. Adolescents identifying themselves as part of skater, hip hop, techno and hippie groups were more likely to use drugs than nerdy, sporty and religious types. The more strongly an individual identified with their group the more they conformed to its norms of alcohol, tobacco and cannabis use.

In an investigation of conformity and prejudice, Crandall *et al.* (2002) found an almost perfect correlation (+0.96) between the degree of prejudice shown towards 105 minority groups and how socially acceptable participants judged each prejudice to be. The minority groups ranged from sex offenders (who attracted most prejudice and were judged most acceptable to be prejudiced towards) to visually impaired people who attracted least prejudice and were felt to be the least acceptable targets of prejudice.

Informational social influence

Informational influence occurs when we conform to majority behaviour because we believe it is right, e.g. because the majority are better informed than us or when the situation is ambiguous – so both private beliefs and public behaviour change. To test this idea participants must be given information about the group's opinion without them having contact (so that we know the influence is not normative, as there is no group to be liked by). Eyssel *et al.* (2006) tested men's conformity to belief in rape myths (e.g. that women enjoy being raped). After rating their acceptance of rape myths and their likelihood of committing rape, the participants were given fictional responses from fellow 'participants' showing either a high or low group acceptance of the myths. When they subsequently rated their likelihood of committing rape, those shown a group norm of high myth acceptance tended to conform to this and rated themselves more likely to commit rape.

Cognitive dissonance

Conformity can alternatively be explained by **cognitive dissonance** – the unpleasant feelings of arousal and anxiety we get when we try to hold in mind two ideas that conflict. Festinger (1957) suggested that when we encounter new information that conflicts with an existing attitude we experience dissonance and can resolve this conflict (and the discomfort) by changing our attitude, i.e. conforming. Some evidence supporting cognitive dissonance cannot be explained by normative or informational social influence. For example, Matz & Wood (2005) found that in a mock jury situation, participants who were told that their opinion of the defendant's guilt differed from the group majority felt anxious, suggesting they were experiencing cognitive dissonance. This declined if they changed their mind, suggesting that their cognitive dissonance reduced because they conformed.

5.3 Milgram's Studies of Obedience

Obedience

When we follow orders from someone we believe has authority over us we are being **obedient**. This is generally good as society functions well when we abide by rules such as driving on the left, but **destructive obedience** is not beneficial. This is when we obey an authority figure who tells us to do something immoral, such as kill someone, and we do so even if it distresses us. Psychological explanations of destructive obedience were sought after World War II to try to understand why ordinary Germans unquestioningly obeyed orders to exterminate millions of Jews. One possibility was that the German people were unusually obedient. Milgram tested this idea, but found that people in general were much more obedient than anyone had anticipated.

Milgram (1963): a study of obedience

Forty male volunteers were recruited using advertisements for a study into the effects of punishment on memory. On arrival at Yale University the real participant and a confederate (who they believed to be another participant) were apparently randomly allocated to the roles of 'teacher' and 'learner'. This was fixed so the real participant was always the teacher. The teacher had to give electric shocks to the learner, using an authentic-looking shock generator, increasing the strength by 15 volts each time a word-pair question was answered incorrectly. No shocks (other than the 45-volt shock given to the real participant to add to the authenticity of the equipment) were actually administered. Participants were also told that 'Although the shocks can be extremely painful, they cause no permanent tissue damage'. The learner indicated severe distress at 300 and 315 volts, then went quiet. If the participant refused to give a shock they were ordered to continue by an experimenter in a lab coat (the authority figure) using a series of verbal prods, e.g. 'The experiment requires that you continue'. Participants were fully debriefed and were followed up a year later.

One hundred per cent of the participants gave shocks up to 300 volts; 65 per cent up to the maximum 450 volts. Many participants were distressed (e.g. 14 showed nervous tension); some of these continued to the end, others ceased to show distress once they decided not to obey. Milgram concluded that people have a strong tendency to obey orders, even ones which distress them and go against their morals, e.g. requiring them to kill a stranger, and that this obedience is due to the situation – the perceived authority – not the participant's personality.

Variations in the procedure

Milgram investigated how different situational factors affected obedience using different locations, proximity between the teacher and the learner, and the appearance and actions of the experimenter and the learner. These confirmed that situational factors (ones present in the environment) are very important in determining the level of obedience (see Figure 5.2). Lüttke (2004) reviewed the findings of replications of Milgram's investigations of situational factors and found that although not all were reliable, two do significantly affect obedience rates: the proximity of the victim (obedience falls when the victim is near and visible) and the presence of obedient or disobedient co-participants (who increase or reduce obedience respectively).

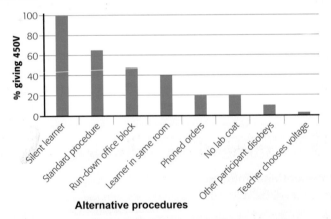

Figure 5.2 Variations in the Milgram procedure and results.

Strengths and weaknesses of the Milgram studies

Milgram's studies have helped us to understand events, such as the Holocaust, by showing the power of destructive obedience. There were strengths to Milgram's method, such as the use of deception, which increased internal validity by ensuring that the participants believed the situation was real, e.g. the 'random' assignment to roles, the authentic-looking apparatus and receiving a test shock. The verbal prods given to participants were fixed so each person received the same orders, increasing reliability. This meant that Milgram's procedure was easy to replicate and replications have mainly produced similar results, although Lüttke (2004) found that changing the experimenter's appearance and using a less respectable location made little difference to obedience rates.

The setting for the study (a university lab) and the task (giving electric shocks to someone) were not situations that people typically come across so the experiment was in some ways artificial and therefore lacking in external validity. However, it did reproduce many features of real-life destructive obedience: the experimenter was a legitimate source of authority, comparable in some ways to a military commander. However, the procedure differed in that the experimenter assured participants that the shocks were painful but not harmful. A Nazi guard, in contrast, would have no doubt that his actions would result in death.

Ethical issues in Milgram's studies

Milgram's study also raised ethical issues, some of which he attempted to solve. Before the study, he asked 14 Psychology students and some of his colleagues how obedient they thought people would be. No one anticipated the levels of obedience or distress he found. The participants were paid $4.50 for attending and were told at the start of the study that this was theirs to keep simply for coming to the laboratory and that the money was theirs regardless of what happened. The participants' **right to withdraw** was, however, severely compromised by the verbal prods, thus they became very distressed (causing psychological harm in the short-term). The participants were **deceived** in several ways, such as about the aim of the experiment, so could not give their **informed consent**. They did, however, meet the learner after the study so saw that they were unharmed, and received a thorough **debrief** – a detailed account of the study – ensuring that participants were returned to their previous state, so that no one (even those who suffered extreme stress) showed any signs of having been psychologically harmed or having suffered any traumatic reactions, according to an impartial psychiatrist's assessment. Less than 2 per cent said they were sorry or very sorry to have taken part.

Later studies of obedience

Hofling *et al.* (1966) tested 22 nurses in a field experiment. They were telephoned on the hospital ward by an unknown doctor and instructed to give 20mg of an unknown drug to a patient (twice the maximum dose). Twenty-two *different* nurses were asked whether they would give a drug in this situation. Twenty-one of the 22 nurses followed the telephone order to give the drug, but only one of those interviewed said that they would. This suggests that although the nurses believed that they would not unquestioningly obey doctors' orders, the majority did so even when this contravened rules or their own judgement. In some ways this is more realistic and therefore has more external validity than Milgram's study as nurses do have to follow doctors' orders. However, these are not generally given by telephone nor are nurses alone on wards or using unfamiliar drugs. When Rank & Jacobson (1975) replicated the study using a known drug (Valium), and the nurses could consult with peers, only 20 per cent obeyed.

Slater *et al.* (2006) used a virtual reality situation to replicate Milgram's procedure using 34 staff and students from University College London who responded to an advertisement. The participants gave a 'learner' avatar word pairs to learn. An experimenter ordered the participant to give increasingly higher shocks when the avatar got an answer wrong, to which the avatar responded with distress. The participants' responses to the stress of the situation were measured. Seventy-four per cent obeyed and gave all 20 shocks, even though their skin conductivity, heart rate and interview responses all indicated that they found hurting the avatar stressful. This suggests that participants respond to destructive orders in virtual reality like they do in real life. There is a strong tendency to obey but to suffer stress as a result.

Figure 5.3 Most of Hofling *et al.*'s nurses obediently gave overdoses of an unknown drug.

5.4 Milgram's Theory of Obedience

Agency theory

Milgram (1974) suggested we need rules to keep society stable and that when we follow orders we surrender some of our free will. He proposed two possible states:

1. *Autonomous state* – we act as we wish to, according to our own free will or conscience
2. *Agentic state* – we relinquish our own wishes and act on behalf of the wider group.

During childhood we are socialised to develop the capacity to enter an agentic state, i.e. to act in the best interests of our society, for example, by following orders from people in authority. If, by acting as an agent of these authority figures, we must do things we find morally objectionable, we experience **moral strain**. This can be reduced by **defence mechanisms** – unconscious strategies that block unpleasant feelings, such as denial.

The agentic state

From a schoolchild doing 'what everyone else wants' even if they would prefer not to, to workers putting employers' demands above their own needs, agency can readily explain obedient behaviour. **Denial** was common both in Milgram's participants and in Holocaust perpetrators who refused to confront what they were doing. Those participants in Milgram's studies who chose to disobey were stressed while making their decision, but not afterwards, as the moral strain was overcome by dissenting.

Strengths of Milgram's theory of obedience

+ *Evidence* suggests that people obey authority figures. Lab experiments such as Milgram's are well controlled, replicable and often highly valid, and field experiments, such as Hofling *et al.*, offer real-world examples.

+ In Blass & Schmitt (2001), people following orders were blamed less than those in authority, suggesting we don't hold people who are being agentic as responsible.

+ Gudjonsson & Sigurdsson (2003)'s questionnaire showed a positive correlation between people tending to follow orders and their use of denial. This supports Milgram's idea that defence mechanisms reduce moral strain.

Weaknesses of Milgram's theory of obedience

− Some of Milgram's *evidence* contradicts agency theory, such as why some participants were disobedient, i.e. it does not readily account for individual differences in obedience.

− Nor can the theory explain individual differences in ability to make others obey.

− Other *evidence* also conflicts with the theory, such as the lack of moral strain in Hofling's nurses even though many knew they had exceeded the maximum dose.

Exam focus

(a) Describe and evaluate Milgram's study of obedience.
(4 marks + 4 marks)

(b) Explain how Milgram's study supports his theory of obedience.
(2 marks)

Examiner commentary

In part (a) the description fails to mention the two key points: measuring obedience by the voltage reached and giving orders using verbal prods, but there's enough correct, detailed material to get all 4 marks. The evaluation is good, except that the last sentence is irrelevant here. Part (b) doesn't answer the question: it describes agency theory – but the last sentence of part (a) would have earned two marks here!

Simon's answer:

(a) Milgram got 40 male volunteers through an ad about a memory experiment. The Ps were artificially selected to be teachers not learners and were shown a false shock machine. They believed they were shocking the learner if he got answers wrong. 65% went all the way but 100% carried on till the learner seemed to be dead. ④ It was good because the Ps didn't know it was on obedience so acted normally and believed the shocks were real so their moral strain was genuine, making it valid. Also, as it was well controlled it could be repeated and the findings have been replicated, so it is reliable. ④ It shows that people follow orders from an authority figure because the experimenter wore a lab coat and the setting seemed real so the Ps entered the agentic state and suffered moral strain, e.g. cried but kept going because they were denying the damage they thought they were doing.

(b) Agency theory says that we can become agentic — acting for the group by following orders, even if it doesn't seem right or autonomous — following what our conscience says. ⓪

Study note

Use the list of BPS guidelines at the top of page 50 to produce a table of the ethical strengths and weaknesses of Milgram's research.

Charisma

Charismatic (or transformational) leadership is an alternative explanation for obedience that considers the skills effective leaders have which encourage others to obey them. Charismatic or transformational leaders are authority figures who are expert at influencing the beliefs, values, behaviour and performance of other people (House *et al.*, 1991). Such leaders are not necessarily nice, just highly effective. For example, Hitler's charisma may have contributed to the obedience in Nazi Germany that permitted the Holocaust.

What makes a charismatic leader?

Early explanations attempted to identify specific personality characteristics of charismatic leaders. More recent research focuses on the social processes by which charismatic leaders obtain obedience from others. These include:

- *personal characteristics* – a high level of communication skills, concern for the needs of 'followers' and impression management (portraying an image of yourself you believe others want to see)
- *social processes* – a clear vision of goals, framing orders in the context of how to reach those goals and using emotive language to provoke action rather than reflection.

For example, Hitler motivated the German people with a vision of a utopian Germany.

Thinking psychologically
Students obey some teachers but disobey others even though they all ought to have the same legitimate authority on the basis of their status. Why might this be?

Strengths of charisma as an explanation of obedience

+ *Evidence* supports the idea, e.g. Den Hartog *et al.* (2007) found a positive correlation between employees' ratings of their managers' charisma and the likelihood of following their instructions: charismatic leaders were more likely to be obeyed.

Weaknesses of charisma as an explanation of obedience

− Charisma is an incomplete explanation since, as Milgram showed, leaders only have to have legitimate authority in order to be obeyed. Milgram's experimenter was not charismatic but still induced high levels of obedience in the participants.

Exam focus

(a) Outline **two** weaknesses of Milgram's theory of obedience. *(2 marks + 2 marks)*

(b) Outline an alternative explanation of obedience and explain **one** way in which it overcomes the problems with Milgram's theory. *(4 marks + 2 marks)*

Carli's answer:

(a) • One weakness of Milgram's theory is that it can't explain why not everyone who has grown up in the same society is obedient. Some of his participants rebelled but it isn't clear why they would have been autonomous rather than agentic.
- Another weakness is that some people are much better at getting people to obey them than others. According to agency theory the only thing that matters is the legitimacy of the authority figure, so individual differences between people shouldn't matter, but they do because we are much more likely to do what some people say if they all represent our society in the same way, e.g. all wearing the same clothes or being the same rank. ②+②

(b) • Charismatic leadership — communication skills, eye contact, needs of followers.
- Social processes — goal-directed orders making people act rather than think. ②+⓪

Examiner commentary

Carli's answer to part (a) is good. She should not have used bullet points but her points are written in full sentences so they answer the question and make sense. In part (b) however, even though there is some relevant material, the brief bullet points mean her answer isn't clear or elaborated so she earns fewer marks. She also needed to answer the second aspect – how this explanation overcomes a problem with agency theory.

5.5 Social Influence in Everyday Life: situational factors and resistance

Non-conformity and disobedience

People don't always conform or obey. When an individual chooses not to conform or obey they are acting **independently**. Some people are more likely to demonstrate independence than others. **Resistance** is an individual's capacity to avoid conforming or obeying when the situation demands these behaviours. Several different factors about the situation, rather than ourselves, affect our ability to resist, including the influence of rebels, reactance and attributions.

Minority influence

Authority figures can influence people through obedience to orders and group majorities can influence them through conformity. However, a minority – or even a single rebel – can also increase resistance. Asch (1955) showed that conformity fell from 37 per cent to 9 per cent if there was a dissenter who gave an answer different from the majority, but one that was also different from the true answer (i.e. a more extreme answer). It fell to just 5.5 per cent if the participant had an ally who identified the correct line. In Milgram's study a rebellious confederate who did not obey caused real participants to be less obedient, whereas obedient confederates increased obedience in participants.

In general, participants in Asch's and Milgram's experiments who conformed or obeyed, altered their behaviour to fit the social demands of the situation without changing their beliefs so were not internalising new beliefs. Moscovici (1985) suggests this is typical of social influence by group majorities and authority figures. In contrast, the power of a rebel works by getting others to internalise new beliefs based on the rebel defying the majority. To do this the rebellious minority must appear committed, flexible rather than rigid and have a consistent, relevant message.

Reactance

When our freedom of choice is deliberately restricted we often respond with anger. Brehm (1966) called the resulting rebellious behaviour **reactance**. For example, a child who is pressured by an adult when told to 'be silent' is likely to make even more noise than one who is told to 'play quietly'. Hamilton *et al.* (2005) compared 13–14 year-olds who were either told that trying drugs was normal but carried health risks (low reactance) or that they must never smoke (high reactance). The low reactance group subsequently smoked less, suggesting that being pressured to surrender one's freedom does result in reactance.

Attribution theory

When we look at other people's behaviour we attribute it to a range of causes; these judgements about the reasons behind what other people do are called **attributions**. We may believe their actions are volitional, i.e. that they have chosen to behave that way. Alternatively, we may think that their behaviour is the product of conforming to group norms (e.g. if lots of people are behaving in the same way), or that they are following orders. If we make attributions of conformity or obedience their behaviour will not have informational influence over us because we conclude they are just doing what they are told. As a result we are less likely to follow suit. This is called **ironic deviance**. Conway & Schaller (2005) showed that in a workplace scenario students were more likely to resist when they disregarded a group norm because they believed it had arisen from the boss's orders.

Figure 5.4 If we think people are doing something – like eating worms – just because they have been told to, we are unlikely to do it too.

5.6 Social Influence in Everyday Life: individual differences

Independence, resistance and personality

In contrast to possible situational factors (page 82), individuals may differ in their ability to resist social pressure. '**Personality**' refers to the aspects of a person that make their behaviour consistent and distinct from that of other people. Some personalities may be more or less able to resist conforming and obeying.

Authoritarian personality

The personality characteristic of **authoritarianism** is related to low independence. An authoritarian personality is politically conservative and hostile, dislikes challenges to authority (from above or below) or deviations from conventional social behaviour and has rigid morals. Authoritarianism was originally proposed to explain the behaviour of the German people during the Holocaust. However, authoritarians exist in many cultures.

Elms & Milgram (1966) compared the personalities of obedient and disobedient participants from Milgram's studies using the **Fascism Scale** ('F Scale': a test of authoritarianism) and a general personality test called the **MMPI**. There were no differences on the MMPI but the obedient participants had higher scores on the Fascism Scale. Altemeyer (1981) reported a study in which participants were ordered to give themselves shocks when they got learning tasks wrong. A positive correlation was found between authoritarianism (assessed using a modern measure, the Right-Wing Authoritarianism Scale) and the shock level reached, again linking obedience and authoritarianism.

Compliant personality

Compliance (see page 76) involves behaving in accordance with the majority behaviour or orders from an authority figure. Gudjonsson (1989) proposed that two personality characteristics make people more susceptible to social influence (**compliant personality**):

1. *Eagerness to please* (because we are likely to do as others do or what they tell us)

2. *Avoidance of conflict* (because a dislike of conflict makes us less likely to defy authority or risk upsetting a majority by deviating from their behaviour).

These factors can be measured on the Gudjonsson Compliance Scale (GCS).

One use of this idea is to understand the ability of suspects to resist pressure to confess to crimes. Gudjonsson & MacKeith (1997) examined the role of compliance in the false confessions of the Birmingham Six, who were arrested following the bombings of two Birmingham pubs in 1974, jailed from 1975 until 1991 then released on appeal. Following their arrest, they were repeatedly ordered to confess by the police and beaten until four of them obeyed. All six men were tested with the GCS in prison. Those who confessed under police orders all scored higher than the two who resisted, supporting the idea that less compliant personalities are more able to resist pressure to obey.

 Exam focus

Describe **one** explanation of how independent behaviour can arise, **other than** locus of control.

(4 marks)

Examiner commentary

Jack has successfully used the idea of a compliant personality – which makes people *less* independent – to explain *more* independent behaviour and his examples add to his elaboration of the explanation, i.e. that this is a legitimate strategy.

Jack's answer:

People with less compliant personalities will be more independent because they are less eager to please and don't care if they are disliked by the group or have to say 'no' to an authority figure. They also don't mind conflict so are more prepared to deviate from the group norm and rock the boat. This also means they will stand up for themselves in the face of an authority figure, e.g. in the Milgram situation they would have disagreed with the experimenter about prods like 'You must continue' and say that they didn't have to. ④

Locus of control

We all tend to have either a broadly internal or external **locus of control**. According to Rotter (1966) people vary between:

- **internal locus of control** – we see ourselves as able to *determine* events
- **external locus of control** – we believe events just happen *to* us.

People with an internal locus of control generally feel more in control of their lives and it is typically linked to healthy behaviour (because internals believe they can make a difference to their own health) and to good mental health (because internals are less anxious and depressed as they feel less threatened and helpless).

Rotter also proposed that people with an internal locus of control are better at resisting social pressure. If we feel we can control situations we are likely to believe that we have a choice to obey or conform, or not.

Strengths of locus of control as an explanation of independence

+ Some *evidence* supports locus of control, for example Brehony & Geller (1981) used an Asch-type conformity test. Those with an external locus were more likely to conform; these participants also had more conformist beliefs about gender roles.

+ In a study on ethics in pharmacy students, Latif (2000) looked for a link between locus of control and level of moral reasoning (the lowest being the belief that blind obedience is morally correct). There was a positive correlation between belief in blind obedience and external locus of control, supporting Rotter.

Weaknesses of locus of control as an explanation of independence

− Twenge *et al.* (2004) investigated the observation that people are becoming less conformist over time. Rotter's idea would predict that in the last 40 years, as people have become more independent, they would also have become more internal. In fact the reverse was true – people have become less conformist but more external.

− Studies such as Latif only measure attitudes to obedience, not obedient behaviour itself, so we cannot be sure that people who *say* that they will be obedient actually will be.

− In other studies the link is very weak. In an investigation of diabetics following doctors' orders, Stewart *et al.* (2000) found only a weak correlation (+0.17) between obedience and external locus of control. This is useful because it is a real-life measure of obedience rather than an artificial one.

Exam focus

Lots of the children at Sally and Beth's school are playing hopscotch, but Sally and Beth both think it is silly so don't join in. An older child, Jill, says they have to. Sally joins in but Beth doesn't.

(a) Outline **one** factor that affects an individual's level of resistance or independence. *(3 marks)*

(b) Explain how the factor you have outlined accounts for the behaviour of **one** person in the scenario. *(3 marks)*

Carl's answer:

(a) Rotter says having an internal locus of control makes you more independent because if you have an internal locus you think you
but if you have an external locus you think ①

(b) Sally could have a compliant personality making her less independent because she would want to please Jill so would obey and would want to avoid getting into an argument with Jill about it. She might also want to be liked by the group of children so would join in. ③

Examiner commentary

Carl's answer to (a) is basic as he has forgotten to go back and fill in the explanations, so it is only worth one mark. If you leave a space to finish an answer later, put a big star by it so you notice as you check through your paper at the end of the exam. In part (b) Carl uses a different explanation from his part (a) answer which is fine in this question as parts (a) and (b) are not linked. He has also followed the instruction to refer to 'one person in the scenario' so part (b) earns 3 marks.

5.7 Social Influence in Everyday Life: social influence and social change

What is social change?

Societies can be described by their social institutions, behaviours, attitudes or relations within the community. When there is an alteration in any of these aspects this is an example of social change. The suffragettes' fight for votes for women or the protests by environmental campaigners would be examples of gradual changes, whilst armed revolutions can create rapid social change. Note how the suffragettes and environmental campaigners were initially minority groups treated as irrational extremists, but both came to represent a majority opinion.

Once the views of the minority are accepted by the majority, conformity exerts social pressure through normative and informational influences on those who resist the social change. If social change becomes law then obedience also comes into play as orders can be issued by authority figures.

Initiating social change

In the early twentieth century the suffragettes defied the majority by demanding the right for women to vote. They had to resist the social pressure to conform to group norms for women of the time and direct orders to stay within their traditional gender role, and not expect equal rights. It is therefore likely that the suffragettes had some of these personality characteristics:

- *low authoritarianism* – they had little regard for authority or tradition
- *low compliance* – they neither avoided conflict nor were eager to please
- *internal locus of control* – they must have believed they had the power to affect events and win the right to vote.

These characteristics are often typical of rebels who initiate social change.

Figure 5.5 Rebels are generally non-authoritarian and non-compliant with an internal locus of control.

The role of resistance and independence

Rebels like the suffragettes may have experienced reactance: being denied what they considered a fundamental right made them angry. Ordering them to stop protesting would have made them more determined. Ironic deviance may also play a role at this point in social change. Once the suffragettes were ordered to conform and to stop demanding the right to vote they may have attributed the conformity of non-suffragettes to this social pressure. If so, the conforming majority would lose their influence over the minority, making the position of the minority stronger.

Minority influence

Although the suffragettes, a minority group, were subject to social pressure from the majority, the reverse effect is important in social change. Milgram and Asch showed that defying authority is easier if you are not the only rebel. The existence of the suffragettes would have made it easier for other people to support women's rights, gradually changing the attitude of the majority. Moscovici suggested that minorities are most effective at causing internalisation (of beliefs) rather than simply compliance (with behaviours) when they are consistent and committed. The suffragettes and subsequent campaigners have shown enormous consistency and commitment. As a consequence, the majority of society has, over the last century, internalised the idea of sex equality.

5.8 Summary

CONFORMITY

In **conformity**, the majority influences the minority. We may **internalise** the beliefs of the majority, so our behaviour changes or we may **identify** with them and change our beliefs or behaviours because we want to be like them. If we change our behaviour but not our beliefs we are merely **complying**.

Asch (1955)

Asch showed that people asked to judge obvious line lengths in the presence of an incorrect majority would comply and answer incorrectly too. However, many knew the answers were wrong so did not internalise.

Normative social influence

Normative influence occurs when we conform to be accepted, or avoid rejection, without changing our beliefs. This explains Asch's findings: the participants probably felt anxious and wanted to be part of the group. Verkooijen et al. found that adolescents identifying with some subcultures (e.g. hippie) were more likely to use drugs than ones identifying with other groups (e.g. religious). The stronger their identification, the more they conformed to the group's drug-use norms.

Informational social influence

Informational influence occurs when we conform to a majority because we believe they are right, so our private beliefs and public behaviour change. Eyssel et al. found that men given fictional responses from other 'participants' with a high group acceptance of rape myths were likely to conform to this belief and to rate themselves as more likely to commit rape.

Cognitive dissonance

Trying to hold two inconsistent beliefs produces **cognitive dissonance** and we experience unpleasant arousal and anxiety. Festinger suggested that dissonance can be overcome by changing our attitude – explaining conformity in some situations. Matz & Wood found that the anxiety felt by mock jurors who were told their decision differed from the majority (so experienced cognitive dissonance) was reduced by changing their decision, i.e. by conforming.

OBEDIENCE

Obedience is following orders from an authority figure. It generally helps society to function well but **destructive obedience** is when we follow orders to do something immoral.

Milgram (1963)

Male volunteers believed they were participating in a study about punishment and memory. The real participant was given (apparently randomly) the role of 'teacher' and a confederate was the 'learner'. The learner answered questions incorrectly and the teacher's obedience was measured by the electric shock level they would give using a real-looking generator. No shocks (except one to the participant to illustrate the equipment) were actually given. The learner shouted at 300 and 315 volts, then went quiet. If the participant refused to give a shock they were ordered to continue by an experimenter (the authority figure) using verbal prods.

All the participants gave shocks up to 300 volts; 65 per cent up to the maximum 450 volts. Many participants were very distressed until they decided not to obey. Milgram concluded that people will obey orders even when this is distressing and that this is due to the situation (the apparent authority) not the participant's personality.

Hofling et al.

This field experiment showed that nurses would follow telephoned orders to give an unknown drug to a patient. Nurses asked whether they would do this said they wouldn't. This study is more realistic than Milgram's as the nurses were on wards and in this situation they do have to follow doctors' orders; but these aren't usually given by telephone, or for unfamiliar drugs nor are the nurses typically alone on wards.

Milgram's variations

Milgram varied situational factors, confirming that they determine the level of obedience, e.g. with a silent learner 100 per cent reached 450 volts. However, Lüttke reviewed other tests of these factors and found only two reliable effects: the proximity of the victim (less obedience with a near and visible victim) and the presence of co-participants (obedient ones increase and disobedient ones reduce obedience).

Strengths of Milgram's studies

Using deception (about the aim, roles and shocks) increased internal validity as the participants believed in the situation. This, the location, and the appearance of the experimenter, made it a realistic reproduction of destructive obedience. The standardised verbal prods increased reliability and made replications possible. These have produced similar results although the experimenter's appearance and location made little difference to obedience (Lüttke).

Ethical strengths included debriefing the participants and meeting the learner, following them up a year later for a psychiatric assessment which demonstrated their long-term health, showing that although there was short-term distress, no ultimate harm was done, so overall the benefits in terms of knowledge gained exceeded any risk of harm to the participants.

Weaknesses of Milgram's studies

The setting and the task of giving electric shocks were artificial, yet it also differed from real situations of destructive obedience as participants were told the shocks were not harmful. The original studies only used male participants so the findings may not have generalised to females.

Ethical weaknesses included denying participants the right to withdraw by using verbal prods and deceiving them in many ways. They were also given $4.50 (although they were assured this was merely for coming to the lab). Harm was a major issue, at least in the short-term, as three participants had seizures and 14 showed signs of stress.

AGENCY THEORY

Milgram suggested that we are obedient when in the **agentic state** (acting for the group). If we are disobedient we are in the **autonomous state** (following our free will). If, by acting as an agent of an authority figure, we behave immorally we suffer **moral strain**, which is reduced by **defence mechanisms** such as denial.

Strengths of Milgram's theory of obedience

Milgram's experiments support his theory as they show that people obey authority figures and experience moral strain. Hofling *et al.*'s field experiment complements Milgram's lab experiments. Blass & Schmitt showed that people following orders (i.e. being agentic) were blamed less than those in authority.

Weaknesses of Milgram's theory of obedience

Some of Milgram's participants were disobedient and agency theory cannot easily explain these individual differences, nor differences in the ability to get others to obey. Moral strain wasn't seen in Hofling's nurses even when they obeyed and knew they had exceeded the maximum dose.

CHARISMATIC (OR TRANSFORMATIONAL) LEADERSHIP

Charismatic leadership suggests that some leaders have skills that encourage others to obey them (House *et al.*). They have personal characteristics such as good communication skills, understand the needs of their followers and impression management. They also use specific social processes to gain obedience, e.g. having a clear vision, giving goal-directed orders and using emotive language.

Strengths of charismatic leadership

Den Hartog *et al.* found that employees' ratings of their managers' charisma correlated positively with how likely they were to follow their instructions.

Weaknesses of charismatic leadership

It is an incomplete explanation of obedience as leaders only need legitimate authority to be obeyed; non-charismatic leaders with the right situational factors will also be obeyed.

NON-CONFORMITY AND DISOBEDIENCE

In everyday life people sometimes choose not to conform or obey and act **independently** – some more often than others, i.e. they are more likely to **resist** social influence. Situational factors also affect resistance.

Minority influence

A minority can increase resistance. Asch found that a rebel who challenged the majority's line judgement caused conformity to fall from 37 per cent to 5.5 per cent. Milgram found that a rebellious confederate caused participants to disobey (and obedient confederates increased obedience). Unlike authority figures and majorities who just affect our behaviour, rebels get others to internalise new beliefs.

Reactance

When our freedom is deliberately restricted we may get angry and rebellious, a process Brehm called **reactance**. Hamilton *et al.* found that teenagers told that trying drugs was normal but risky (low reactance) smoked less than ones told they must never smoke (high reactance).

Attribution theory

We find reasons for other people's behaviour called **attributions**. If we judge them to be conforming or be obedient they won't have informational influence over us so we are less likely to do the same thing than if we believe their actions are independent. This is called **ironic deviance**. Conway & Schaller found that students were more likely to resist a group norm when they believed it was due to people following their boss's orders.

INDIVIDUAL DIFFERENCES

There may be differences in independence because some **personalities** are more able to resist conforming and obeying.

Authoritarian personality

The **authoritarian personality** is linked to low independence. They are hostile, respect (and expect) authority and dislike unconventional behaviour. This was proposed to explain behaviour during the Holocaust but authoritarians exist in many cultures.

Elms & Milgram compared the personalities of obedient and disobedient participants from Milgram's studies and found that obedient participants were more authoritarian. Altemeyer reported that participants in a study who were ordered to give themselves shocks, who were more authoritarian, were also more likely to give themselves stronger shocks.

Compliant personality

Gudjonsson suggested that compliant people are more eager to please others and to avoid conflict so are more susceptible to social influence. Gudjonsson & MacKeith found that the four of the Birmingham Six who were forced to give false confessions had higher compliance scores than the two who resisted the police orders.

Locus of control

Rotter suggested that we have either an **internal locus of control** and feel we can determine events or an **external locus of control** and believe things happen to us. People with an internal locus feel in charge of their lives so can resist social pressure as they believe that they have a choice about obeying or conforming.

Strengths of locus of control

Brehony & Geller found that people with an external locus were more likely to conform in an Asch-type conformity test and had more conformist beliefs about gender roles. Latif found a positive correlation between belief in blind obedience and external locus of control.

Weaknesses of locus of control

Twenge *et al.* found that although people have become more independent in the last 40 years they have also become *less* external. Many studies providing evidence for locus of control and obedience (e.g. Latif) only measure *attitudes* to obedience so the findings may not apply to real obedient behaviour. Some studies find only weak relationships, e.g. Stewart *et al.* found a correlation coefficient of +0.17 between obedience to doctors' orders in diabetics and their external locus of control.

SOCIAL CHANGE

Gradual changes in behaviours, attitudes or relations within the community are often the product of minority influence, such as the suffragettes or environmental campaigners.

Rebels and social change

The suffragettes were typical of a minority which changes the majority. To succeed in their demand for women's right to vote they are likely to have been low in authoritarianism (with little regard for authority), low in compliance (e.g. embracing conflict) and have had internal locus of control (to believe they could change voting rights).

Reactance and social change

Rebels like the suffragettes were angered by the denial of a fundamental right so reactance would have increased their rebellion. When individuals recognised that orders to conform (and accept being vote-less) were responsible for the conformity of non-suffragettes, the conforming majority would lose their influence, making the position of the minority stronger. This is one way that ironic deviance can promote social change.

Minority influence

The suffragettes were consistent and committed so would have influenced the majority by causing internalisation (of beliefs) rather than simply compliance (with behaviours).

Majority influence and obedience

Once the majority accepts the minority view, normative and informational influence can cause conformity in those still resisting the change. If social change becomes law, orders are issued from sources of legitimate authority so obedience also comes into play.

5.9 Social Psychology Scenarios

Scenario 1: Angie the artist

Conformity

When Angie goes to university everybody seems to be wearing special trainers. After a week she hasn't really found any friends and she doesn't want to seem different so she goes and buys some trainers like everyone else's, even though she finds her old ones more comfy.

Using your understanding of social influence, explain the processes responsible for Angie's behaviour.

Obedience

Angie is studying Art History and is told by one of the students on her course that she needs to go to a museum in a town miles away to see some original pieces for her next essay. Angie doesn't want to go because it means she would miss her grandma's birthday lunch. However, her lecturer tells her she has to go, so she misses the birthday lunch even though she knows this will really upset her grandma.

Describe how Milgram's studies and theory can help to explain Angie's behaviour in relation to the student on her course and her lecturer.

Independence and resistance

The university has a fund-raising week and Angie gets involved with producing a joke book. She is a good artist and designs the cover, and draws illustrations for some of the events being held. However, when she sees the contents, some of the jokes are really offensive and she refuses to let her artwork be used. The editor (a lecturer) tells her she cannot drop out now and she must allow them to use her work. She still says no.

Use your understanding of independence and resistance to suggest possible reasons for Angie's response.

Revision note

When you are giving longer answers remember how important it is to elaborate on what you are writing. You might do this with examples, studies or additional details.

Scenario 2: Sam the social changer

Minority influence and social change

Sam is protesting to get the local battery chicken farm closed down. He is a vegan; he never eats any animal products, he doesn't have a pet and he doesn't wear leather shoes. Every single weekend he is in the town centre giving out leaflets he produces himself. He's there regardless of the weather or how much he'd rather be indoors watching the television.

Use your understanding of factors affecting social influence to explain why Sam is likely to be effective in instigating social change.

Rebels and social change

At school Sam is often in trouble because he disagrees with teachers if they say things he doesn't think are fair. He has been excluded for a week for setting the school hamster free. When everyone else is tucking into special treat of turkey for school Christmas lunch, Sam insists on only eating sprouts. He started up a recycling club to collect waste paper from around the school. He kept collecting it and piling it up outside the headmaster's office until he gave in and let Sam arrange for it to be collected by a recycling company.

Identify the factors in the description above that suggest Sam would be an effective rebel likely to promote social change.

For **one or more** of these factors, present evidence to illustrate how the factor(s) can influence behaviour.

Majority influence and obedience

Sam begins to win over lots of the local people. His school only serves free-range meat and eggs, and many shops are refusing to stock battery eggs or chicken. Sam is hoping to extend his influence and insist that the school puts a ban on any battery farmed food being consumed on the premises – even if students have brought it in themselves.

Use your understanding of conformity to explain why more local people are likely to accept Sam's thinking as time goes on.

If Sam succeeds in changing the school rules, what source of social influence would then come into play and how effective is it likely to be?

Study note

The section on social change draws on ideas from many areas in the social influence topic. Draw a mind-map or spider diagram to illustrate the links between the different areas of social psychology and reasons for social change.

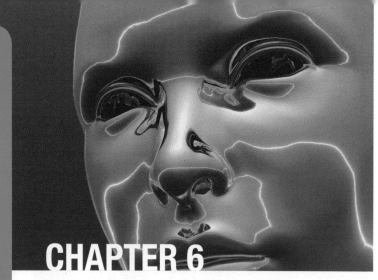

CHAPTER 6
Individual Differences

6.1 An Introduction to Individual Differences

YOU NEED TO:

know what these terms mean:

- abnormality
- deviation from social norms
- deviation from ideal mental health
- electroconvulsive therapy (ECT)
- psychoanalysis
- systematic desensitisation (SD)
- cognitive behaviour therapy (CBT)

describe and evaluate:

- how abnormality has been defined
- biological approach to psychopathology
- psychodynamic approach to psychopathology
- behavioural approach to psychopathology
- cognitive approach to psychopathology

understand and apply your knowledge about the treatment of abnormalities, including:

- biological therapies: drugs and ECT
- psychological therapies: psychoanalysis, systematic desensitisation and cognitive behavioural therapy

KEY TERMS

abnormality a psychological state indicating mental disorder on the basis of emotions, cognitions and/or behaviour. It may be defined in different ways, e.g. as a deviation from social norms, from ideal mental health or as a failure to function adequately

deviation from social norms a definition of abnormality based on the individual exhibiting behaviour which differs from that of most members of their society and which others find socially or morally unacceptable

deviation from ideal mental health a definition of abnormality which uses indicators of psychological well-being such as high self-esteem, personal growth, coping, being independent and having an accurate perception of reality

electroconvulsive therapy (ECT) a biological therapy for depression using a small, short electric shock to the brain which causes a brief seizure

psychoanalysis a 'talking cure' devised by Freud as a therapy for patients with psychological problems that did not appear to be biological in origin. Important processes in analysis are free association, catharsis, transference and reparenting. The analyst provides the patient with an interpretation of their current problems in relation to their childhood traumas, early relationships and unconscious processes

systematic desensitisation (SD) a therapy based on the behavioural approach, which uses classical conditioning. Patients (e.g. with phobias) are exposed step-by-step to an anxiety hierarchy of more frightening stimuli whilst a relaxed state is maintained by the therapist. Through this they unlearn the association between the object or situation and fear

cognitive behaviour therapy (CBT) a way to help patients to identify and change irrational thoughts which makes their feelings and behaviour more positive

6.2 Defining Abnormality

Abnormality

An assessment of **abnormality** must decide whether an individual's behaviour, emotions or cognitions are normal or not. This decision needs to be accurate for ethical and practical reasons. It is unethical to label people inappropriately (e.g. if they are just eccentric or rebellious). Correct diagnosis is essential if people are to receive appropriate care.

Deviation from social norms

A **social norm** is a belief or behaviour that most members of a society hold or do. Some people behave differently or hold alternative views. Most differences are harmless but behaviour that opposes the moral values of the whole society is seen as indicating abnormality. People with a diagnosis of antisocial personality (psychopaths) are impulsive, aggressive and irresponsible. A key symptom is a failure to conform to social norms of lawful behaviour, leading to frequent arrest. Other **deviations from social norms** leading to diagnoses of abnormality include sexual attraction to children (paedophilia) and animals (zoophilia).

Figure 6.1 When does eccentric behaviour become abnormal?

Personal liberty and social control

Defining abnormality using deviation from social norms is problematic as it restricts freedom of choice. Historically, diagnoses for people whose behaviour defied social norms illustrate this, such as drapetomania (slaves 'irrationally' wanting to escape), moral insanity (women 'irrationally' wishing to keep inherited wealth) and homosexuality. Such diagnoses enabled a powerful group (white, middle-class males) to maintain social control over women, black people and gay people by limiting their freedom and imposing 'treatments' we would now call punishment.

Cultural variations in social norms

Social norms are culturally specific. This causes problems for psychiatrists working with people from different groups from themselves (e.g. ethnic, socio-economic or age). As a consequence differences exist in the rates of diagnosis, e.g. in the UK, Black and Irish people are more likely to be diagnosed with a mental disorder than people from other ethnic groups (Littlewood & Lipsedge, 1997). This discrimination is both unfair and suggests that deviation from social norms is imperfect as a way to define abnormality, e.g. causing problems in multicultural societies where there are several conflicting social norms.

Exam focus

One way to define abnormality is using deviation from social norms.

(a) Outline this approach to defining abnormality. *(4 marks)*

(b) Explain **one** weakness of this approach. *(2 marks)*

Declan's answer:

(a) A social norm is a standard of behaviour that most people in a group do. Conformity means people in a society hold the same beliefs, e.g. most people would think washing and going to work every day was right but killing people was wrong. However, there might be times when it was okay, like in self-defence. But Milgram showed that normal people can break social norms due to obedience. ①

(b) If we say people are abnormal if they don't conform to social norms we might make mistakes and start calling people without problems abnormal just because they are a bit odd. ①

Examiner commentary

Declan's answer to part (a) earns a mark for explaining what is meant by a social norm in relation to mental health, but doesn't say how this approach is used to tell us what is *ab*normal rather than normal so the answer is rudimentary. He also wanders off the point at the end. What he has written for part (b) is correct but also very limited – this needed elaborating.

Failure to function adequately

Abnormality can be defined by being unable to cope with the tasks of day-to-day living. Many people experience problems, such as feeling sad or unmotivated, but when these are so persistent or severe that the individual has difficulty with their daily life they may receive a psychiatric diagnosis. An alternative is to decide whether the person can live a 'normal' life. For example, we all have fears, both sensible and irrational, but these are only abnormal (i.e. a phobia) if the individual avoids the situation or becomes distressed by it such that this interferes significantly with their normal routine, occupation, social life or relationships. This is useful as it offers a clear distinction between unusual and abnormal, and takes into account the individual's welfare as well as social norms.

The Global Assessment of Functioning

DSM-IV-TR uses the **Global Assessment of Functioning** (GAF) scale to assess adequacy of functioning. A score is given from 1 (extreme difficulty functioning, e.g. suicidal or in persistent danger of hurting others) to 100 (functioning well, with problems never getting out of hand). This indicates how much help a patient needs and how urgently.

Adequacy and personal freedom

It is difficult to judge when an individual's behaviour is inadequate. Again, the decision could affect personal freedom. Someone who leaves their job and comfortable home to live in primitive, dangerous conditions may appear not to be functioning adequately. However, they may be more fulfilled as an environmental protester camping out to preserve a habitat or as an aid worker in a war zone than when living 'normally'.

DSM

The **Diagnostic and Statistical Manual of Mental Disorders** (DSM) is a means to assess and classify mental disorders. The current version (DSM-IV-TR, 2000) is currently under revision and the (already controversial) DSM-V is planned for release in 2012.

Ideal mental health

Jahoda (1958) used the analogy of good physical health (e.g. feeling energetic and having a normal temperature) to understand mental health. She suggested abnormality is when we fail to meet the criteria for **ideal mental health** including: having high self-esteem, personal growth (fulfilling one's potential), coping with stress, being independent, having an accurate perception of reality and environmental mastery (being effective in relationships, work and leisure and at adapting to change).

This measure of **deviation from ideal mental health** is a value judgement of the ideal self and many people may never attain this kind of mental health. It is, however, helpful in guiding the need for and focus of therapy, e.g. to build self-esteem, handle stress or improve relationships. Defining abnormality in this way is unlikely to restrict personal freedom. Jahoda's criteria (except perception of reality) are reasons why people seek help rather than have it imposed on them.

Cultural variations in ideal mental health

Jahoda's ideas, based on the UK and US in the 1950s, now – with a global perspective – seem **culture-bound**. Collectivist cultures (e.g. in Asia and Africa) place less value on independence, and instead see people as functioning successfully when they are highly interdependent with their family and community. Personal growth is also a culture-bound concept as the ideal of striving for personal success is not widely valued in much of the world so would not be a useful indicator of mental health.

Thinking psychologically

Imagine people who are: too tired to get out of bed, can't make decisions because they have thoughts which are not their own, terrified to go out of the house, threatening to let themselves be killed by a digger uprooting an ancient forest. How would each of the definitions of abnormality evaluate their mental health?

6.3 Biological Approach to Explaining Psychopathology

The biological model

Our biology affects our mind and behaviour so is important in understanding possible causes of and treatments for abnormality. The **biological approach** suggests that abnormalities in the nervous system, our genetic make-up (**genotype**) and the biological environment can be important in mental illness (an aspect of our **phenotype**).

Genetics

Genes are rarely the sole cause of mental disorders but they do affect vulnerability, i.e. the risk of developing a mental disorder. If we have a genotype that makes us susceptible to **schizophrenia** and our environment or experiences add to this risk (e.g. by using recreational drugs) our biological predisposition to schizophrenia may become apparent.

Studying genetic influences

The pattern of mental disorder running in families could be explained by inheriting a predisposition. Alternatively, children may acquire symptoms from their family through parenting or conditioning (see pages 98 and 100). Adoption and twin studies attempt to separate the effects of genes and family environment. Heston (1966) found that adopted children whose birth mothers had schizophrenia were more likely to have schizophrenia themselves as adults, suggesting that genes affect vulnerability.

The biological environment

Environmental influences are not just psychological. Biological factors such as drugs and infections may also play a role in mental illness. Bembenek (2005) found that people who developed schizophrenia were more likely to have been born to mothers who were in the middle of their pregnancy during a flu epidemic. Geddes *et al.* (1999) found several factors that related to a higher risk of developing schizophrenia in adulthood, such as being a premature baby or needing an incubator, suggesting that schizophrenia may be associated with oxygen starvation at birth.

Neurotransmitters

Abnormal levels of some neurotransmitters are linked to mental illness. In depression the levels of serotonin and noradrenaline are low. In schizophrenia, dopamine levels are high. As neurotransmitter levels may be genetically determined, genes could affect vulnerability to mental disorder. Dannlowski *et al.* (2007) found abnormal variations in two genes affecting serotonin processing in patients suffering from depression.

Brain abnormalities

In schizophrenia the left half of the brain (controlling the right side of the body) does not function normally. Purdon *et al.* (2001) found that untreated patients with schizophrenia had weaker right (but not left) hands than controls; a difference which disappeared after treatment. This suggests that schizophrenia involves a problem with the left brain, which antipsychotic drugs can correct.

 **Exam focus**

Explain how the biological model can account for psychological abnormality.

(6 marks)

Jodie's answer:

Drugs, the flu and a lack of oxygen are environmental factors that can give people mental illnesses. This is because they can affect the way our body works, like the brain, neurotransmitters and genes. Things like serotonin, dopamine and noradrenaline matter too. ②

Examiner commentary

Jodie knows lots of relevant words but has only given a basic answer. She is right that the first three are important factors but she doesn't say why – and 'give' implies they are solely responsible, which is unlikely. Jodie needed to give an *explanation* of the model in order to earn more marks.

6.4 Biological Approach to Treating Psychopathology

Drug treatments

As some mental disorders are linked to abnormal neurotransmitter levels, the symptoms may be controlled by drugs which attempt to return these levels to normal.

Drugs for depression and schizophrenia

Selective serotonin reuptake inhibitors (SSRIs) are antidepressants which slow down the recycling of serotonin so the neurotransmitters can restimulate the receptors. **Noradrenaline reuptake inhibitors** (NRIs) work in a similar way. As people with depression tend to have lower than normal levels of these neurotransmitters, this can treat their symptoms. However, different drugs are needed as individual patients vary in their response to **antidepressants** in terms of effectiveness in reducing symptoms and side effects. For example, NRIs are useful for motivating patients whose depression has left them inactive.

Phenothiazines (e.g. chlorpromazine) were early **antipsychotics** (for schizophrenia) which had very general effects and blocked the action of dopamine at the synapse. As people with schizophrenia have higher than normal levels of dopamine, this reduces symptoms. Newer antipsychotics (e.g. clozapine) have narrower chemical effects (so have fewer side effects).

Effectiveness of drug treatments

The effectiveness of drug treatments at reducing symptoms is measured in a **random control trial** with a **placebo** condition. Arroll *et al.* (2005) compared such trials for **tricyclic** and SSRI antidepressants. Improvement was seen in over half of the patients treated with antidepressants but under half of those receiving a placebo. SSRIs took longer to work than tricyclics but had fewer side effects. In general, drugs help many patients, but not all.

Ethical issues in the use of drugs

Drugs work, but they may not be the best choice. Pinquart *et al.* (2006) found that antidepressants were less effective than psychological therapies for depression. Drugs are cheaper and can be given instantly, but there is usually a waiting list for therapy.

Side effects

Drugs can have side effects. Although less severe for newer drugs, serious problems still occur. For 0.05 per cent of patients on antipsychotics, **neuroleptic malignant syndrome** (which can lead to brain damage) can arise and antidepressants can produce serotonin syndrome, which can (although rarely) cause long-term neurological problems (Adityanjee *et al.*, 2005). Antipsychotics can damage the immune system, depress mood and lead to **tardive dyskinesia** (uncontrollable limb and facial movements).

 **Exam focus**

'Some drugs for depression can increase the risk of suicide in the early weeks of treatment. Others cause physical problems like excessive tiredness.'

Evaluate the usefulness of drug treatments for psychological abnormality. *(6 marks)*

Sanjeev's answer:

Drugs for depression and schizophrenia work by decreasing levels of serotonin and increasing levels of dopamine. SSRIs block the action of serotonin and antipsychotics inhibit the reuptake of dopamine so more floats around in the synaptic gap. Newer drugs do this more exactly than older ones so are better. ②

 Examiner commentary

Sanjeev has mainly described how drugs work instead of evaluating them – even though there was a hint in the question stem about side effects. He earns 2 marks as, although much of the answer seems irrelevant, his answer is at the top of the lowest marking band because he's saying that drugs work so is *implying* they are useful. Without the last comment about newer drugs being better – which *is* evaluative – he would only have scored 1 mark. Note that Sanjeev has muddled up the changes in neurotransmitter levels – serotonin is *low* in depression and dopamine is *high* in schizophrenia; the effects Sanjeev describes for drugs would make the patients worse.

Electroconvulsive therapy (ECT)

ECT is mainly used to treat depression. An electric shock is given to the patient's head for a fraction of a second. This causes a seizure, lasting 15–60 seconds, similar to that experienced in epilepsy. Shocks are usually **bilateral** as this is thought to be more effective than **unilateral** ECT, although it is also more likely to lead to side effects. ECT is repeated 6–12 times in total over two or more weeks.

Modern ECT uses small shocks (e.g. 800 milliamps) given for short periods (e.g. one second), given under anaesthetic and with drugs to paralyse muscles, preventing broken bones.

Effectiveness of ECT

Eranti *et al.* (2007) found that 59 per cent of depressed patients treated with ECT were symptom-free immediately after treatment, and a month later, compared to only 17 per cent of controls. However, after six months most patients had relapsed, suggesting that ECT is only effective in the short-term.

Ethical issues in the use of ECT

A major side effect of ECT is memory loss. It is usually temporary but is cumulative so worsens over a course of treatment. Lisanby *et al.* (2000) found that in the week of treatment, patients experienced significant forgetting, especially those who had received bilateral ECT. After two months their personal memories had largely recovered but their impersonal memories were still worse than the controls.

Patients should consent to treatment but it is doubtful whether those with severe depression (who may benefit most from ECT) can understand what it involves. Also, around 2000 patients a year in Britain are given ECT without their consent, under the Mental Health Act. Furthermore, according to Rose *et al.* (2003), only about half of ECT patients feel they had enough information before their treatment. Given the side effects, the problems with obtaining informed consent raise serious ethical questions. Of course there may be situations where the potential ethical and psychological costs are worth the risk, if, for example, the patient may commit suicide if ECT is not administered.

Study note

When you are describing the strengths and weaknesses of any ideas that can be compared (such as theories, research methods or experimental designs) it is useful to consider whether the strengths of one indicate weaknesses of another. For example, think about whether drugs cause memory loss or ECT increases the risk of suicide.

Exam focus

'Severely depressed patients are sometimes offered ECT.'

Outline the risks of ECT and explain what can be done to ensure that ECT treatment meets ethical guidelines.

(6 marks + 6 marks)

Alan's answer:

In ECT 'treatment' people had strong electric shocks to their brain making them convulse, bite their tongues and break bones because the muscles contract so hard. This was done without anaesthetic and could burn their brains. They also lost their memory. Even nowadays it still causes headaches and memory loss for a week or so though Lisanby found that eight weeks after treatment most people were okay at remembering where they lived and other things about themselves, but still couldn't remember general things like the names of everyday objects. AO1 = ⑤, AO2 = ⓪

Examiner commentary

Alan has accurately described the main risks associated with historical and modern ECT procedures and his AO1 mark has enough detail to just reach the top band. To improve this further he could have given some commentary about the risks, e.g. how memory loss can become worse with repeated treatments. Alan scores no AO2 marks at all because he has not answered the second part of the question. He needed to suggest ideas such as providing information about the procedures and risks so that patients can give their informed consent (although this is difficult when we don't know how ECT works or how severe side effects will be), giving patients muscle-relaxants, using unilateral shocks when possible and so on.

6.5 Psychodynamic Approach to Explaining Psychopathology

The psychodynamic model

The **psychodynamic approach** was developed by Freud who believed that although some mental disorders were biological in origin, many were the result of psychological factors such as poor early relationships and traumatic childhood experiences.

Early relationships and mental health

Psychodynamic psychologists believe that a child's developing personality, both normal and abnormal, is affected by their relationship with their parents. Freud suggested that in childhood different aspects of the relationship with parents matter and that, as adults, we may regress to the stage during which we had relationship problems. In the **oral stage** (0–1 year), children are forming their first close relationships. Problems with these can lead to later difficulties such as over-dependence on others (e.g. **dependent personality disorder**). In the **anal stage** (1–3 years) the child experiences parental authority so conflicts, e.g. over potty training, can lead to adult problems such as being excessively orderly. Freud believed that some anxiety disorders (e.g. **obsessive-compulsive disorder**) may arise at this time. Massie & Szajnberg (2002) found that poor childhood parental relationships and traumatic events in childhood were linked to poor adult mental health.

Early trauma and mental health

According to psychodynamic psychologists, traumatic experiences in childhood can lead to abnormality. This is because emotion (like physical energy) can only be transformed or discharged, it cannot 'disappear'. Negative emotion resulting from childhood trauma therefore remains in the mind and can later be transformed into symptoms. Freud proposed that depression often results from loss (e.g. of a parent) in childhood. **Conversion disorders** arise when a psychological problem leads to a physical symptom such as being unable to speak or move. Kanaan *et al.* (2007) scanned the brain of a patient with a conversion disorder causing weakness on the right side of her body (which is controlled by the left side of the brain). When asked about a traumatic life event she denied it was important, but a brain scan showed a reduction in activity in her left motor cortex.

Anna O

Breuer & Freud (1896) described a conversion disorder in Anna O: her deafness, neck paralysis and limb numbness were caused by negative emotions from being caught listening at her parents' door while they had sex, and being unable to use her intellectual abilities. These emotions were transformed into physical symptoms in adulthood because of the death of her father.

Strengths and weaknesses of the psychodynamic approach

Whilst it is supported by some detailed evidence, much of it comes from Freud's self-analyses, informal observations and interpretations of what his patients said in therapy, which may have been biased and unrepresentative and would now be considered unscientific. There is little evidence for some of Freud's ideas, such as the oral and anal stages, e.g. little evidence links the anal stage to obsessive-compulsive disorder.

Exam focus

Tick true **or** false for each statement.   *(3 marks)*

	True	False
1. Losing a parent during childhood increases the risk of adulthood depression.		
2. Experiencing trauma in childhood always leads to mental illness.		
3. Psychodynamic psychologists view genes as more important than experiences.		

Examiner commentary

The correct answers are: 1 True, 2 False, 3 False. The psychodynamic approach doesn't say that childhood trauma *always* leads to mental illness and sees experiences as more important than genes.

6.6 Psychodynamic Approach to Treating Psychopathology

Psychoanalysis

Psychodynamic psychology offers a '**talking cure**' for people with mental health problems. **Psychoanalysis** is the most intensive (4–5 sessions a week) and long-term (for several years). In psychoanalysis the patient (**analysand**) sits or lies comfortably and **free associates**, i.e. says whatever comes into their mind, e.g. childhood memories, dreams, current life situations and feelings towards the analyst. The analyst interprets the links between past experience, symptoms and patient/analyst relationship.

Early experience and catharsis

The psychodynamic approach suggests we are unconsciously affected by early experiences. Psychoanalysis aims to enable us to remember, re-experience and safely work through these experiences to discharge the emotion experienced as a result of a trauma – a process called **catharsis** (an important factor in all psychological therapies).

Early relationships and transference

In psychoanalysis, the patient may play out their relationship with key people (e.g. parents) in their behaviour towards the analyst – this is called **transference**. This is important as it gives insight into early relationships so interpretation of transference is a key technique. Analysts therefore encourage transference, giving away little about themselves. By giving the patient feedback about how their current relationships are distorted by their early relationships, the analyst helps the patient to understand their problems.

Reparenting

A benefit of having a good relationship with a responsible adult in psychoanalysis (the analyst) is to '**reparent**' the patient. For patients who have never had a good-quality relationship this is a vital aspect of therapy. Analysts therefore keep clear boundaries to sessions, e.g. never being late or cancelling sessions so they are 'model adults'.

The effectiveness of psychoanalysis

Eysenck (1952) reviewed studies of psychoanalysis and found that 44 per cent of psychoanalytic patients improved compared to 66 per cent who improved with 'spontaneous remission', i.e. no treatment at all, and that therefore no treatment is better than psychoanalysis. However, this study itself had some weaknesses, such as a biased sample which included studies with weak methodology showing poor outcomes for analysis but excluding studies with better methodology that showed good outcomes. Also, only a complete cure was counted as 'improvement' in analysis, but small benefits were scored as improvements in control patients. Finally, the time taken to recover was not considered, so untreated patients whose symptoms declined over years were counted as equivalent to patients whose symptoms declined in weeks during analysis. Bergin & Garfield (1978) reanalysed Eysenck's data and estimated that around 80 per cent of patients in analysis and 30 per cent with no treatment significantly improved. More recently, Leichsenring & Leibing (2007) reviewed 24 studies of psychodynamic therapies including nine of psychoanalysis. Twenty-three of these showed that the therapies (including psychoanalysis) were as effective as the other standard therapies.

Ethical issues in psychoanalysis

Although psychoanalysis is effective its use is declining in Britain, especially in the NHS, because it requires frequent sessions over a long period of time so is not cost-effective. A minority of patients may really need such intensive treatment but most can benefit from quicker, and hence cheaper, therapies. Daily sessions of psychoanalysis (plus travel time) disrupt patients' lives and they may find that their insight into the effects of their relationship with their parents makes their current relationships worse. Also, psychoanalysis is not suitable for patients who are not articulate.

6.7 Behavioural Approach to Explaining Psychopathology

The behavioural model

Unlike psychodynamic psychologists who explore the unconscious mind, behaviourists focus on observable behaviour. The **behavioural approach** is concerned with the learning of behaviours through experience, such as the acquisition of abnormal behaviours through **classical conditioning**.

Classical conditioning

Prior to conditioning there must be an unconditioned stimulus (US) that already produces an unconditioned response (UR) and a new stimulus (the neutral stimulus, NS) that does not produce a response. An association between these stimuli develops when the US and NS repeatedly occur together. Once conditioned, we respond to the NS (now called the conditioned stimulus, CS) as we did to the US. This new response is called the conditioned response (CR).

Classical conditioning can explain mental disorders in which the main symptom is a response to a stimulus. In **phobias** we respond to objects or situations with fear and in **paraphilias** (sexual fetishes) we respond with sexual arousal. Both can, at least in some cases, be explained by classical conditioning.

Watson & Rayner (1920): Little Albert

An infant was repeatedly shown a rat (the NS), which he had been unafraid of, and each time he reached for it, a loud noise was made (the US), which scared him (UR). After just two days, Albert leaned away from the rat when it was presented and after a week it made him cry, as did other white fluffy things like cotton wool and a Father Christmas beard. Although the pairings stopped after seven days, Albert was still afraid after seven weeks.

Phobias and paraphilias

Little Albert was classically conditioned to fear something that did not hurt him: the rat. Similar processes could explain how we come to have irrational fears, i.e. a phobia. An innocuous (neutral) stimulus might become accidentally associated with a genuinely unpleasant US, such as if you get stung by a buzzing bee you become frightened of all things that buzz, even though most of them are harmless.

In paraphilias we associate a US (e.g. an attractive member of our target sex) with an NS (e.g. particular music or a school uniform). Just as little Albert's fear generalised to other objects, a learned sexual response to school uniforms might become generalised to schoolgirls. This is a partial explanation of paedophilia. This is why Britney Spears and Baby Spice from the Spice Girls caused such controversy by adopting aspects of a schoolgirl-like appearance, such as wearing pigtails.

Exam focus

One explanation of abnormal behaviour suggests that it is learned. Use appropriate terms from the list below to complete the diagram to show how a child could develop lepidopterophobia (a fear of butterflies).

You will need to use **one or more** terms more than once. *(6 marks)*

- Unconditioned stimulus (US)
- Conditioned stimulus (CS)
- Unconditioned response (UR)
- Conditioned response (CR)
- Neutral stimulus (NS)

Butterfly (_ _) ➡ happy

Run after a butterfly (_ _) + fall over and break an arm (_ _) ➡ fear (_ _)

Butterfly (_ _) ➡ fear (_ _)

Examiner commentary

The correct answers in order are: NS, NS, US, UR, CS, CR.

6.8 Behavioural Approach to Treating Psychopathology

Systematic desensitisation

Classical conditioning underlies **systematic desensitisation** (SD), a therapy used to unlearn conditioned responses, e.g. phobias. Jones (1924) treated a boy (Little Peter) with a phobia of rabbits by slowly bringing a caged rabbit closer to him until he could touch it. This gradual increase in the level of the fear-arousing stimulus (exposure) is the basis of systematic desensitisation. Another key process is relaxation. We cannot be relaxed and afraid at the same time, so if the patient stays calm when faced with the thing they fear they will become desensitised. The therapist may use muscle relaxation, hypnosis, meditation or anti-anxiety drugs like Valium to keep the patient calm while working through an **anxiety hierarchy**. This is a sequence of steps from a mild to the most feared stimulus, which the patient agrees with the therapist. A patient with a fear of mice might start looking at a picture of cartoon mice, work through touching a toy mouse to letting a real mouse run over them – by which time they have overcome their phobia.

Newman & Adams (2004)

MV, a 17-year-old boy with a learning difficulty, was afraid of dogs. He was trained to relax using breathing exercises and focusing his gaze away from dogs towards his mother. In therapy his anxiety hierarchy began with photos of dogs then worked through dogs which could not reach him, were unleashed and were unfamiliar. Although this worked at first, 18 months later he was still phobic. Further sessions focused on staying relaxed at the higher end of the hierarchy especially in the most feared situation – meeting unfamiliar dogs off their lead in a park. At the end of 26 sessions this was successful.

The effectiveness of systematic desensitisation

Newman & Adams' findings show that SD can treat phobias and there are many similar cases. Paraphilias can also be treated with SD. Martz (2003) described the SD of a woman who could only orgasm using the dangerous practice of autoerotic asphyxiation (self-strangulation). In ten therapy sessions she repeatedly wrote about autoerotic asphyxiation while not sexually aroused, so unlearning the association between the sexual response and asphyxiation. Behavioural treatments of paraphilias also use masturbatory reconditioning so that the patient learns to become aroused in response to normal sexual stimuli. This patient used a vibrator to achieve orgasm without asphyxiation.

Case studies alone are not sufficiently scientific to confirm the effectiveness of a therapy so evidence from studies with control conditions is needed. Brosnan & Thorpe (2006) desensitised 16 technophobic students over ten weeks. At the end of their IT course their anxiety about computers was significantly lower than a control group who had not received SD. Zettle (2003) used SD for students with a fear of maths; they had reduced levels of anxiety unlike a control group who were not desensitised.

Ethical issues in systematic desensitisation

Behavioural therapies to treat phobias raise ethical issues because they have to expose patients to the source of their fear so make them anxious. However, if they are effective they also have the longer-term gain of reducing fear, so there is a balance between effectiveness and ethics, i.e. the benefits of treatment would exceed the ethical costs. SD is less traumatic than other behavioural treatments which cause patients more anxiety but are often more effective. **Flooding** is the most traumatic, involving exposing patients to the thing they fear in an extreme form for a small number of long sessions. A mouse-phobic might be shut in a room with loose mice for 2–3 hours. Choy *et al.* (2006) reviewed evidence about the effectiveness of flooding and found it was better at tackling phobias than SD but that many patients were so traumatised that they left therapy sessions or did not return.

6.9 Cognitive Approach to Explaining Psychopatholog

The cognitive model

The **cognitive approach** focuses on the role of abnormal thinking patterns that typically exist in patients with particular disorders. For example, anxious people see the world as threatening whilst depressed people see it as hopeless and unrewarding.

Ellis's ABC model

Ellis (1977) proposed the **ABC model** to explain how the influence of pre-existing irrational beliefs caused people to overreact to negative life events with anxiety or depression. Palmer & Dryden (1995) used the ABC model to explain a student's response to failing an exam: A (the activating event) is failing the exam, B (the beliefs) might be, 'I cannot bear not passing', leading to C (the consequences for mental health) of depression.

Abrams & Ellis (1996) identified two types of irrational belief that matter to our mental health: **musturbation** is the tendency to think that we *must* succeed in everything, making us very sensitive to failure; **I-can't-stand-it-itis** is the belief that when something does not go smoothly it is a disaster, making us overreact to minor problems.

Beck's negative thinking

Beck (1976) explained the relationship between negative thinking and depression by recognising three types of negative thinking common in people with depression. **Negative automatic thinking** occurs because negative views of the self, the world and the future (the **cognitive triad**) tend to reinforce one another, making it difficult for a depressed person to see good things in themselves or others, or the possibility of these improving. Beck also suggested that in depression, we attend to the negative aspects of a situation and ignore the positives. This causes an overestimation of the 'downside' of any situation so we come to more negative conclusions. **Self-schemas** contain our information about ourselves, e.g. our beliefs and feelings, and are used to interpret new information about ourselves. If this set of beliefs is based on criticism from our parents we will have **negative self-schemas**. These would lead us to feel badly about ourselves and to interpret new situations negatively. For example, if we think we are boring and a disappointment but somebody is nice to us we might believe they simply pity us rather than are enjoying our company.

Cognitive vulnerability

Both Beck and Ellis suggested that some thinking patterns put us at risk of anxiety and depression; this is called **cognitive vulnerability**. Koster *et al.* (2005) tested the selective attention of depressed people to positive, neutral and negative words (e.g. 'powerful', 'crane', and 'loser', respectively). They found that depressed participants took much longer to disengage from words like 'loser' than non-depressed ones suggesting that they do focus more on negative stimuli.

Manipulating cognitive vulnerability

Armfield (2007) demonstrated the role of cognitive vulnerability in anxiety in relation to thoughts about the predictability, controllability and dangerousness of spiders. Arachnophobic students were shown a picture of a spider and asked to imagine putting their hand against an aquarium containing a spider. Different groups were told the spider had a painful bite (high danger) or that it could not bite (low danger); that they could remove their hand if the spider approached it (low uncontrollability) or that they had to keep their hand still (high uncontrollability); or that the spider made sudden movements (high unpredictability) or not (low unpredictability). When assessed again for spider phobia the participants in the high uncontrollability, high danger and high unpredictability conditions were most afraid of spiders. This shows that people's thoughts about one specific (imagined) spider affected their fear of spiders in general, i.e. that our beliefs make us more or less cognitively vulnerable to anxiety.

6.10 Cognitive Approach to Treating Psychopathology

Cognitive behavioural therapy

Cognitive behavioural therapy (CBT) is the most commonly used psychological therapy. It usually takes place once a week or fortnightly for between five and twenty sessions. CBT helps patients to identify irrational and unhelpful thoughts and tries to change them. As our thoughts affect our feelings and behaviour, making our thinking more positive should make us feel better.

Approaches to CBT

There are different varieties of CBT, using different techniques to change unhelpful ways of thinking. Ellis's approach focuses on identifying unhelpful beliefs and vigorously arguing against them. Beck's approach uses reality testing experiences to challenge irrational beliefs and counter them, e.g. asking someone who believes they never enjoy socialising to go out and find something they enjoyed about the experience, then write about it in a diary. Therapists tend to use a blend of such techniques and may combine these with behavioural therapies, e.g. a patient who is afraid of loud noises might be asked to desensitise themselves by finding places to go, like a shooting range, to expose themselves to the source of their fear.

The effectiveness of CBT

Butler *et al.* (2006) reviewed many studies of CBT and concluded that it was very effective for treating depression, generalized anxiety, panic disorder, social phobias, post-traumatic stress and childhood depressive and anxiety disorders. It was also moderately effective for marital distress, anger and chronic pain. The Royal College of Psychiatrists recommends CBT as the most effective psychological treatment for moderate and severe depression.

However, not all evidence is positive, especially for CBT used to treat conditions other than depression and anxiety. Sandahl *et al.* (1998) found that 15 months after different treatments for alcohol dependency, more patients were abstaining following psychodynamic therapy than CBT. Evidence from review studies can also be criticised. Harrington *et al.* (1998) observed that several reviews of CBT failed to consider studies where CBT did not work, biasing the results in favour of CBT. Most studies on CBT have also focused on short-term gains for patients with symptoms of only one condition. It may be less effective in the long-term or for patients with a range of symptoms.

Ethical issues in CBT

CBT involves altering patients' cognitions, so the therapist could potentially determine how the patient thinks – which is open to abuse. A responsible therapist would negotiate any changes with their patient and only use techniques to make changes that the patient wanted. However, Ellis's brand of CBT raises ethical problems as it is very directive, telling people how they should think. For example, if a patient is suffering work-related stress because they believe their employers are working them too hard, a therapist using Ellis's approach might identify this as an irrational belief. If the patient's employers were abusing the rights of their workforce the use of CBT might allow this malpractice to continue.

Trower & Jones (2001) found that CBT practitioners in Britain generally saw Ellis's style as too directive. Ellis's approach is more popular in the USA where there is a cultural emphasis on individual responsibility. Neenan suggests that Ellis's aggressive approach is offensive in Britain, not just because it places responsibility on the patient rather than their environment so could be politically misused, but also because it is impolite, and the British have a tremendous emphasis on politeness.

6.11 Summary

ABNORMALITY

Abnormality can be defined in different ways so it is important to get the decision right for ethical reasons (to avoid incorrect or unjust labelling) and practical reasons (to ensure appropriate diagnosis and care). Mental disorders are classified using DSM.

Deviation from social norms

Most members of a society hold shared views and behave in similar ways. **Deviation from social norms** can indicate abnormality, e.g. in antisocial personality disorder or sexual attraction to children or animals.

Assessing social norms

Defining abnormality using deviation can restrict freedom of choice. Historically, some people who defied social norms, e.g. women wanting rights to wealth, were diagnosed with mental illnesses and could be socially controlled. Psychiatrists may not make accurate diagnoses outside their social/cultural group, leading to discrimination.

Failure to function adequately

Failure to function adequately can indicate abnormality, e.g. too depressed, afraid or confused to cope with daily tasks. This definition clearly separates unusual and abnormal behaviour and considers the individual's welfare.

Assessing failure to function adequately

DSM-IV-TR uses the GAF scale to assess a patient's functioning to guide how much and how urgently they need help. However, individuals may appear inadequate because they are expressing an individual choice, which could limit the personal freedom of people who are more fulfilled living outside mainstream ways.

Ideal mental health

Indicators of **ideal mental health** include high self-esteem, personal growth, coping with stress, independence, perceiving reality accurately and interacting effectively with the social and physical environment. Abnormality is a failure to meet these criteria.

Assessing ideal mental health

Collectivist cultures see being socially interdependent rather than independent as successful and personal growth as less important than Western societies, so these concepts are **culture-bound** and unhelpful in indicating mental health. It is a value judgement so may be difficult or impossible to attain.

THE BIOLOGICAL MODEL

The **biological approach** says that abnormalities in the nervous system, our genes and our biological environment play a role in mental illness.

Genetics

Twin and adoption studies show that genes affect the risk of mental disorders (but are not the sole cause). Genetic factors affect vulnerability (e.g. via neurotransmitter levels) increasing the risk of mental illness if exposed to particular environments or experiences.

Biological environment

Biological factors, e.g. drugs or infections, are environmental factors that play a role in mental illness. Pregnant women exposed to flu are more likely to have children who develop schizophrenia later, as are babies deprived of oxygen at birth.

The nervous system

Depression is linked to low levels of the neurotransmitters serotonin and noradrenaline; schizophrenia with high dopamine levels. Brain abnormalities are also linked to mental illness. In some cases of schizophrenia the left half of the brain does not function normally but some physical symptoms can be controlled with antipsychotic drugs.

DRUG TREATMENTS

Drugs can correct abnormal neurotransmitter levels in some mental illnesses. SSRIs increase the availability of serotonin in people with depression and treat their symptoms. Some drugs for schizophrenia block the action of dopamine and reduce symptoms.

ELECTROCONVULSIVE THERAPY

ECT is a treatment for depression which uses a very mild, brief bilateral electric shock to the brain that causes a seizure. This is given under anaesthetic with muscle relaxants and is repeated 6–12 times over two or more weeks.

Effectiveness of drugs

Many drug treatments are effective as assessed in random control trials compared to a placebo. Such trials show that drugs vary in the time they take to work and their side effects and that any particular drug does not help all patients.

Effectiveness of ECT

ECT reduces the symptoms of depression in the short-term but patients relapse quickly. However, it causes memory loss (especially if bilateral), which builds up over treatment.

Ethics in drug use

As drugs work it is important to make them available, but they are sometimes less effective than psychological therapies (e.g. for some people with depression). However, drugs are cheaper and instant. Side effects can cause serious neurological problems, e.g. neuroleptic malignant syndrome (from antipsychotics) and serotonin syndrome (from antidepressants).

Ethics and ECT

It is used as a last resort treatment for patients whose depression has not responded to other treatments and are at risk of suicide, but they are least likely to be able to give informed consent to treatment. Many patients are also given ECT without their consent under the Mental Health Act.

THE PSYCHODYNAMIC MODEL

The **psychodynamic approach** suggests that not all mental disorders are biological but may result from poor early relationships and traumatic childhood experiences.

Early relationships

Freud suggested that a child's relationship with their parents relate to adult problems as we may regress to the stage in which we had relationship problems. So problems with a child's first relationship (in the oral stage) can lead to dependent personality disorder and a child who conflicts with parental authority (in the anal stage) may later develop Obsessive Compulsive Disorder.

Early trauma

Traumatic experiences in childhood can lead to abnormality because negative emotions are transformed into symptoms, e.g. emotions from the loss of a parent in childhood can cause adult depression. In conversion disorders, negative emotions lead to physical symptoms such as paralysis.

Evaluating the psychodynamic approach

Freud used self-analyses and interpretation of patients' comments in therapy. This evidence may be biased and unrepresentative. Little evidence supports ideas such as the oral and anal stages or links to mental illnesses such as OCD.

PSYCHOANALYSIS

In **psychoanalysis** the patient free associates, giving descriptions of the present and past which are interpreted. By safely re-experiencing and working through early experiences the negative emotions are discharged – the beneficial process of catharsis. The patient may play out early relationships, e.g. with parents, in their behaviour towards the analyst (transference) providing insight which can help the patient to understand the effect of early problems on their current relationships. The stable relationship with the therapist can help to 'reparent' patients who lacked this in childhood.

Effectiveness of psychoanalysis

An early review by Eysenck suggested that psychoanalysis did not help patients but this study used biased sampling, measures of 'improvement' and time taken for 'improvement'. Bergin & Garfield reanalysed the data and found that psychoanalysis was better than no treatment.

Ethics and psychoanalysis

Psychoanalysis is effective but intensive and long-term so is not cost-effective and is declining as although a minority of patients may need it, most can benefit from quicker, cheaper therapies. Also, the intensity of psychoanalysis is disruptive to patients' lives.

THE BEHAVIOURAL MODEL
The **behavioural approach** suggests that abnormal behaviours may be learned, e.g. through classical conditioning.

Classical conditioning
This takes place when an existing stimulus (the US), which already produces a response (the UR), is associated with a new stimulus (the NS), which does not. After repeated pairings the NS becomes a CS and produces the same response (now called the CR). This can explain how phobias and sexual fetishes (paraphilias) are learned.

Phobias and paraphilias
Little Albert was conditioned to fear a rat by associating it with a frightening noise, so other phobias could be acquired in the same way. In paraphilias a classically conditioned response to a member of the target sex may be inappropriate or the learned response may generalise to inappropriate stimuli (such as children or animals).

SYSTEMATIC DESENSITISATION
Systematic desensitisation (SD) is a therapy which uses classical conditioning. Phobic patients are gradually exposed to an anxiety hierarchy of increasingly fear-arousing stimuli. They are kept calm, e.g. using hypnosis, and since we cannot be relaxed and aroused at the same time, they overcome their phobia by unlearning the fear response.

Effectiveness of systematic desensitisation
Case studies show that both phobias and paraphilias can be treated with SD. However, these are not sufficiently scientific to confirm the effectiveness of a therapy. Experimental studies comparing SD to control conditions also show that desensitisation, e.g. for technophobia and fear of maths, is effective.

Ethics and desensitisation
Behavioural therapies must balance their effectiveness against exposing patients to their fears and raising ethical issues. Flooding causes patients more anxiety than SD but is also more effective – although the trauma may cause patients to drop out of flooding therapy.

THE COGNITIVE MODEL

The **cognitive approach** suggests that mental illness is caused by abnormal thinking patterns, e.g. anxious people focus on threat and depressed people on the negative things. These are examples of how cognitive vulnerability and dysfunctional thinking patterns put us at risk.

Ellis's ABC model

Ellis suggested that irrational beliefs about negative life events lead to depression and anxiety. These irrational beliefs include musturbation, which makes us sensitive to failure, and I-can't-stand-it-itis, which makes us overreact to minor problems.

Beck's negative thinking

Beck identified three types of thinking in people with depression: negative automatic thoughts occur because negative views of the self, world and future (the cognitive triad) reinforce one another so it is hard to view things positively; selectively attending to the negative aspects of a situation causes us to reach negative conclusions, and negative self-schemas lead us to interpret new situations negatively.

Cognitive vulnerability

Some thinking patterns put us at risk of anxiety and depression; this is called cognitive vulnerability. Evidence shows that beliefs about situations do affect our cognitive vulnerability to phobias, supporting the idea that thinking determines mental health.

COGNITIVE BEHAVIOURAL THERAPY

Cognitive behavioural therapy (CBT) is the most common psychological therapy. Sessions are less frequent and the duration of therapy is shorter than in psychoanalysis. It identifies and challenges patients' irrational thoughts in order to change them. Ellis's approach argues vigorously against unhelpful beliefs. Beck's approach uses reality testing of irrational beliefs. Therapists may combine these and use behavioural therapies, e.g. SD.

Effectiveness of CBT

CBT is very effective for depression, anxiety and social phobias and works for other conditions too. It is recommended as the best psychological treatment for depression. However, CBT is less effective for conditions other than depression and anxiety, e.g. for alcohol dependency psychodynamic therapy is better. Furthermore, review studies may take biased samples; most studies only consider short-term gains and single-symptom patients so long-term effectiveness and use with multiple-symptom patients may be poorer.

Ethics and CBT

As CBT can alter patients' cognitions it is open to abuse if therapists do not negotiate changes and techniques with the patient. Ellis's approach also raises ethical problems as it tells people how they should think. This could be misused (e.g. by unscrupulous employers) and, in Britain, it is considered impolite as the techniques are so confrontational.

6.12 Individual Differences Scenarios

Scenario 1: What will happen to your friends?

Abnormality

Ivan has lots of friends at university. As they say their farewells he wonders what will happen to them all. Ten years later many are living fulfilling lives. Kim has a great job but struggles to cope most of the time. She thinks people are getting at her even when they aren't and feels that nothing she does is ever good enough, even though she's a top-grade scientist. Benny has moved abroad and found his perfect job; he lives entirely on his own in a lighthouse on a rock miles from anywhere. He doesn't wash or cut his hair. He doesn't talk to anyone for months at a time, even though he could do so. Mary used to run a department at the council but can't any more because she hears voices that tell her not to go to the office because it is bugged. Stan loves his job as a zookeeper working with elephants, but is terrified of the spiders that spin great big webs all over the elephants' indoor space.

Describe **two or more** ways of defining abnormality.

Use the definition(s) you have described to explain why **two** people from the scenario above might be classified as abnormal.

Explain why one of the people above might be **incorrectly** classified as abnormal.

Strengths and weaknesses of definitions

Much later in life, Ivan and his partner have two daughters, Nicola and Emily. Both become psychologists. Nicola feels very strongly that there is a need for people to conform to the standards that society expects. Emily travels the world studying other cultures and believes that we place too much emphasis on Western standards.

In terms of definitions of mental health, describe the views that Nicola and Emily are likely to hold.

Nicola and Emily come home at Christmas and argue about the merits of their definitions of mental health. Describe how each daughter might defend her opinion about how abnormality should be defined.

Scenario 2: Biology or background

Nature versus nurture

Sol and Graham are identical twins. They grew up with their brother Richard who was adopted when they were all seven years old. They are now adults and all three suffer from depression. Graham and Sol are also very frightened of storms and if there is thunder and lightning they are embarrassed about how afraid they feel.

Using your understanding of factors that affect mental illness, explain why all three boys have depression.

Explain why it is unlikely that the same explanation can account for depression in Sol and Graham as for Richard.

Strategies

One winter before Richard was adopted there was some very severe weather. The twins' father used to get very angry when they got out of bed to watch the wind and rain lashing the windows. If they were found out of bed watching a storm they were beaten.

Using your understanding of factors affecting mental illness, explain why only Sol and Graham are upset by storms.

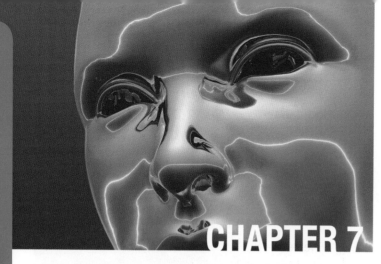

Studying and Revising

CHAPTER 7

Your course and your exams

This chapter aims to help you to acquire good study habits during your course and to help you to prepare effectively for your examinations. Ultimately you will have to demonstrate what you have learned in just three hours in response to just a few questions. You need to be sure that you can make the most of your time.

The examinations

You will take two 1 hour 30 minute exams for the AS-level examination, each worth 50 per cent of the total AS mark. They may be in the same or different sessions (January and/or June). The Unit 1 exam covers cognitive and developmental psychology and research methods; the Unit 2 exam covers biological and social psychology and individual differences.

Assessment objectives

In each exam there will be questions to test each **assessment objective** (AO). These are:

AO1: testing knowledge and understanding, e.g. how well you can recognise, recall and understand psychological ideas and whether you can select, organise and communicate relevant information. This is tested with questions such as multiple-choice, true/false, fill-in-the-gaps and short- or longer-answer questions asking you, among other things, to:

- **identify** = name
- **select** = choose the correct option
- **define** = say what is meant by
- **outline** = give brief details without explanation
- **describe** = give a detailed account without explanation.

AO2: testing application of knowledge and understanding, e.g. how well you can analyse and evaluate ideas or apply them to situations. This is tested with questions which ask about the validity, reliability or credibility of information and ones using terms such as:

- **evaluate** = assess the value or effectiveness of
- **analyse** = examine in detail
- **explain** = give an account of why and how
- **discuss** = give a reasoned, balanced account
- **apply** = explain how something can be used.

AO3: testing your knowledge of how science works, e.g. whether you can describe safe, ethical and practical techniques for investigating psychology and understand and evaluate the methodology and findings of investigations.

A few command words ask for a mixture of assessment objectives, most often AO1 and AO2. These include '**discuss**' and '**critically discuss**'. Their exact meaning will depend on context but 'discuss' is used to ask you to describe and use your understanding, e.g. to evaluate or apply it, 'critically discuss' wants you to describe and evaluate (in terms of strengths and weaknesses). '**Compare**' and '**critically compare**' also demand both AO1 (to outline two things: research methods, theories, explanations, and so on) and AO2 (to consider ways in which they, or their strengths and weaknesses, are similar and different).

Unit 1

Cognitive psychology: models of memory, eyewitness testimony and strategies for memory improvement.

Developmental psychology: attachment and day care.

Research methods: methods and techniques, designing investigations and analysing and presenting data.

Unit 2

Biological psychology: stress, coping and stress management.

Social psychology: social influence (conformity and obedience), independent behaviours and social change.

Individual differences: psychopathology (abnormality), definitions, explanations and therapies.

On course: good study habits

In order to be able to answer questions effectively in exams you need to be able to:
- understand the relevant information
- be able to recall it
- be able to use it effectively.

There are things you can do throughout your course to help yourself in each of these aspects.

Understanding psychology

Although your teacher will have explained each topic in class you might have been absent, not concentrating, not grasped it very well or simply have forgotten it. Here are some things you can do to improve your understanding:

- *Reread your notes*: look back through your class notes regularly to check that you still understand them. Try to do something active with them, like writing a list of the key terms, theories and studies to use as a checklist for later. If, on rereading, your notes don't make sense, ask your teacher for help, ask a friend or look the topic up.

- *Read your textbook*: use the index to find the right page – don't just flick through the book.

- *Read a different textbook*: it may contain the same information but it will be explained in different ways, which can help you to both understand and remember ideas better.

- *Talk about psychology*: if you find an example in everyday life, on television, in a book or elsewhere, that relates to your course, tell someone! Explaining how the psychological concepts apply will help you to become more familiar with the ideas.

- *Keep your notes organised*: sorting them out will help you to understand each topic: thinking about what the key ideas are, which theories are important and what evidence relates to each one. Use a copy of the specification so you can see how each topic is broken down – all except research methods basically have 'content' which is applied to everyday life. Make sure that you have notes on everything in the specification (yours is AQA–A 2008). If you haven't been given a copy, find it at: **www.aqa.org.uk/qualifications.html**.

- *Write a word list*: using the specification construct a word list, adding new terms as you encounter them (or you could use the glossary in this book). Write out your own definitions for them and give an example where possible.

- *Practise answering exam questions*: try to use a range of different question types, both in question type and for AO1, 2 and 3.

Active learning

One of the best ways to help yourself is to make your learning active; you need to do more than just read. Here are some suggestions for things to try:

- *Questions and answers*: pair up with a friend who also studies Psychology. Choose a small topic each (e.g. describing a study or evaluating a theory) and, using your notes or a textbook, write a set of questions and answers. Use these to test each other.

- *Flash cards*: using questions and answers as above, write them onto cards, so the question is on one side and the answer on the other. Use them to test yourself, or get a non-psychologist (e.g. someone in your family) to help you – or you could record yourself saying them!

- *Draw it out*: lots of aspects of psychology can be represented in pictures or tables. Use big sheets of paper to make posters for your walls (e.g. of models of memory, types of attachment, the Strange Situation, types of graphs, positive and negative scattergrams, the body's stress response, sources of stress, Milgram's study, how drugs work, and so on.

- *Spot the difference:* try comparing two theories, studies, research methods or therapies. In what ways are they similar and in what ways are they different?

- *Circle time*: draw several concentric circles on a large piece of paper. Write a concept in the middle and elaborate on it in each circle, e.g. with descriptions, evidence and applications.

Ready to recall: effective revision

If you keep your notes organised and complete during your course, revision will be easier. But if like many students you haven't quite managed it, good revision techniques can still help.

For revision to be really effective it needs to be well planned. You need enough time and must be sure it is well spent. The two key elements are:

1. Identifying what you have to know and learning it
2. Identifying how you will be tested and practising it.

The examiner is looking for very specific things. Your responses should be *accurate*, appropriately *detailed* and *elaborated* and you should answer the question *effectively* (rather than flawed, basic and brief). This means knowing your stuff and explaining it well.

Time management

- *Start revising early*: the AS-level Psychology exams are often at the very start of the spring term and before the half-term holiday in the summer.
- *Organise your revision*: allow yourself enough time to revise everything you need to. There's no point in being great at one topic or unit when you know nothing about the rest.
- *Use your time well*: spread out your revision, work in 'chunks' of time (e.g. a whole morning) but have breaks too. If you think you are time-wasting, do a time circle.

Revision timetables

A revision timetable can just be a list of topics with target dates. Spending a whole day drawing up an exotic (and doubtless improbable) one is unlikely to be a good use of time. Take into account that you will have other commitments and be realistic, e.g. about how much you can do on a Saturday, or when your favourite television programme is on. Also consider how well you understand each topic – you may need more time for some. One way to decide this is to go through the specification using highlighters and 'traffic light' the topics: green = know and understand well, orange = know and understand fairly well, red = knowledge and understanding is less good.

You then need to stick to your plan to ensure you get all the topics done.

Time circles

If you are not keeping to your plan, stop and work out how much time you intended to spend revising the previous day. Then work out how much time you actually spent on each activity using Figure 7.1. Draw two time circles and use them to decide whether you could be more efficient; but remember, this isn't a substitute for work!

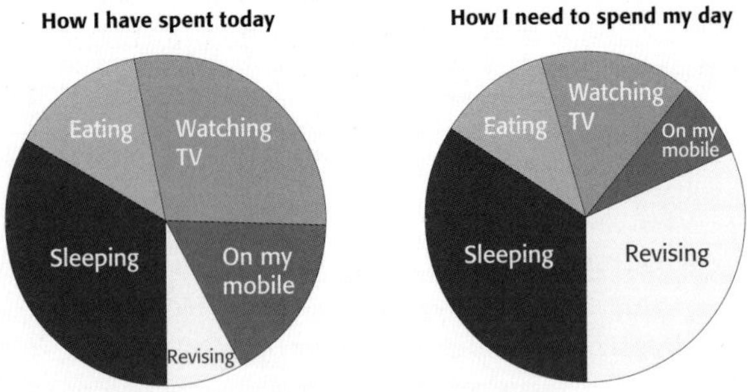

Figure 7.1 Plan your time using time circles.

Motivating yourself

Revision can be dull because the material seems familiar, even if you haven't learned it fully. This and the sheer volume of it can be demotivating. Here are some pointers to help:

Do:

- set achievable, intermediate, goals
- reward yourself when you finish a session – you will have hopefully earned it!
- give yourself regular breaks – they will help you to concentrate in the long run
- entertain yourself by doing your revision on coloured paper or with coloured pens (or to music *if* you can concentrate)
- work with a friend or get someone to read you questions or answer them out loud
- have a dedicated work space (e.g. a corner of your room) so you keep your revision separate.

Don't:

- give up too easily – meeting a target will motivate you
- try to work with the television on a programme you want to watch as it will distract you. Turn it off or have a break and work properly in another time slot
- spend time on distraction activities like making an all-colour revision timetable or re-filing your notes when you should actually be revising.

Knowing what you need to know

If you haven't used a copy of the specification to organise your notes, use one to ensure that you revise everything that you need to.

The specification tells you what you need to learn. Bear in mind however that examination questions can present you with information, such as studies or scenarios, that you haven't encountered before. You need to be able to use your understanding of psychology to answer the question(s) that are asked.

Sitting the examination

Be sure that you know the date, time and paper that you are sitting. Plan your travel so that you will arrive in good time. Take a black pen and at least two spares. Do not take your phone into the exam hall – it is not allowed: it is not enough for it to be turned off; you cannot have it with you.

Tackling questions

Read each question carefully. So many candidates lose marks because they answer what they *think* the question says, when it's actually asking something different. Some students find underlining keywords in the question helps. If you prefer some questions to others you can do those first, but be sure that you spend enough time on the rest of the paper.

Mark allocation: look at the number of marks for a question. Bear this in mind when you write your answer; spend longer on and write more for questions which earn more marks.

Numbers: pay attention to questions that say the *number* of things you should write about, e.g.:

Outline **two** problems with observational studies.   *(2 marks + 2 marks)*

If you only outline one problem you can only get half marks. If you do more than two you will only earn marks for two of the problems you describe.

Either/or: some questions say to do *either* one thing *or* another. You will only get marks for doing one of the alternatives. For example, if a question asks: 'Describe one disadvantage of **either** field experiments **or** natural experiments' you will not earn any more marks for describing a disadvantage of each.

Making references to a scenario or stem: some questions begin with a 'stem' (a short introduction) or a 'scenario' (a description of a real-life situation). This is there to help you and you may use this information in your answer. However, if the question specifically asks you to refer to the stem or scenario in your answer you must do so to access the full range of marks. Consider this scenario:

Fred is so stressed about being bullied at work that it is making him very depressed. He was picked on at school and finds it hard to cope with all kinds of social situations.

This might be followed by two different questions:

(a) Describe **one** stress management technique that could be used to help Fred.

(b) Describe how **one** stress management technique could be used to help Fred.

The first question is asking you to describe a technique *without* applying it to Fred (though if you did that wouldn't necessarily be wrong). In the second however you *must* apply the technique to Fred. Another way this type of question can be asked is: 'With reference to the scenario above…' which makes it very clear that you need to mention the text in your answer.

Parted questions: if a question is divided into parts (e.g. (a) and (b)), write your answer in parts too. If you don't the examiner will divide it up for you – and this may not be to your advantage! Sometimes parts of a question are related. If a question asks you to describe something, for example, describe a sampling method in part (a) and evaluate it in part (b), you must use the *same* sampling method in both parts. If you use a different one in part (b) you will score zero for that part of your answer.

Combined AO questions: some questions are designed to test two assessment objectives. Try to make sure that you provide both aspects of the required response in your answer. For example, 'Compare biological and social psychological explanations of aggression.' would require you to both give some description of the explanations (AO1) and to indicate similarities and differences between them (AO2).

Glossary

A

ABC model – an explanation suggesting that pre-existing irrational beliefs cause people to overreact to negative life events with anxiety or depression

abnormality – a psychological state indicating mental illness on the basis of emotions, cognitions and/or behaviour. It may be defined in different ways, e.g. as a deviation from social norms, from ideal mental health or as a failure to function adequately

acoustic – related to sound, e.g. acoustic encoding is the use of sound-based representation of information in a memory store

acute – short-term (e.g. of stress)

adoption study – a technique used to separate the effects of genes and family environment. Children brought up by a non-biologically-related family are compared to both their biological and adoptive families

adrenal cortex – the outer region of the adrenal glands, which release hormones involved in the stress response, including cortisol and aldosterone

adrenal glands – a pair of endocrine glands lying above the kidneys. Each are like two glands: the adrenal medulla produces adrenaline and the adrenal cortex produces cortisol

adrenal medulla – the inner region of the adrenal glands, which release substances involved in the stress response, including the hormone adrenaline and the neurotransmitter noradrenaline

adrenaline – a hormone produced by the adrenal medulla in response to a stressor. It has effects such as increasing the heart rate

adrenocorticotropic hormone (ACTH) – a hormone from the pituitary gland which acts on the cortex of the adrenal glands causing the release of the hormone cortisol

agency theory – an explanation for obedience proposed by Milgram (1974) which suggests that we follow orders because we have been socialised to enter the agentic state

agentic state – a mental condition in which, according to agency theory, we surrender our free choice over our behaviour and obey an authority figure in order to act on behalf of the wider group, i.e. as 'agents' of society

aim – the purpose of an investigation, which is generally expressed in terms of what the study intends to demonstrate

aldosterone – a hormone from the adrenal cortex which keeps the blood pressure high

amnesia – profound memory loss

anal stage – second stage of Freud's psychosexual theory of development (2–3 years) during which a child's focus is on its anus

analysand – the person receiving psychoanalysis

antidepressants – drugs used to treat depression, anxiety and eating disorders, including SSRIs and NSRIs, monoamine oxidase inhibitors (MAOIs) and tricyclics

antipsychotics (neuroleptics) – drugs used to treat schizophrenia and related conditions

antisocial personality disorder – the failure to conform to acceptable standards of lawful behaviour as indicated by repeatedly performing acts that are grounds for arrest

anxiety hierarchy – a graded sequence of fear-arousing stimuli developed between a client and a therapist in preparation for systematic desensitisation

anxiolytics – drugs used to treat anxiety disorders

AO1 – an assessment objective which tests knowledge and understanding, i.e. whether you can recognise, recall and understand psychological ideas and can select, organise and communicate relevant information

AO2 – an assessment objective which tests the application of knowledge and understanding, i.e. how well you can analyse, apply and evaluate information (e.g. in terms of validity, reliability or credibility)

AO3 – an assessment objective which tests your knowledge of how science works, i.e. whether you can describe safe, ethical and practical techniques for investigating psychology and understand and evaluate the methodology and findings of investigations

assessment objective (AO) – a skill being tested in an examination. There are three at AS level: AO1, AO2 and AO3

attachment – a close two-way emotional relationship between two people such as a child and a parent. An attached infant stays close to its carer (*proximity seeking*) and uses them as a secure base from which to explore. When separated they get anxious (*separation distress*) and they distrust unfamiliar adults (*stranger anxiety*)

attribution – the judgement an individual makes about the reasons for the behaviour of other people, e.g. whether we believe they have chosen to act in a particular way or whether they are doing so because of conformity (i.e. because they are following the group) or obedience (i.e. because they are following orders)

authoritarian personality – an individual characteristic which is related to low independence. Such individuals gain high scores on the Fascism Scale (although score no differently from others on general personality tests such as the MMPI) and tend to have rigid morals, are hostile and dislike challenges to authority and deviations from conventional social behaviour

autoerotic asphyxiation – a dangerous sexual practice in which partial strangulation is used in an attempt to heighten arousal

automatic thoughts – see *negative automatic thinking*

autonomic nervous system (ANS) – this is part of the peripheral nervous system, i.e. it lies outside the central nervous system (CNS). The neurons of the ANS transmit messages around the body to all the vital organs

autonomous state – a mental condition in which, according to agency theory, we act as we wish to, governed by our own free will or conscience

avatar – a computer-generated representation of a person, e.g. in a virtual reality environment

avoidant attachment – (Type A) an insecure attachment type where children do not seek proximity, show secure base behaviour, become distressed in the carer's absence or display a positive reuniting response

B

behavioural approach – an area of psychology which focuses on, and uses explanations (e.g. of abnormality) based on, observable behaviour. It suggests that we learn (and can unlearn) behaviours through experience, such as through classical conditioning

behavioural categories – specific events in the participants' stream of activity which are independent and operationally defined

bilateral – both sides, e.g. an electric shock given to both sides of the head in ECT

biofeedback – a stress management strategy. A client receives ongoing data about their body functions, e.g. pulse rate, blood pressure or muscle tension. This information indicates tension or relaxation so can help a client to learn to become more relaxed. Initially, the client cannot deliberately change their state, but the feedback helps them to become aware of the way their thinking and behaviour affect their biological functioning

biological approach – an area of psychology which focuses on, and uses explanations (e.g. of abnormality) based on, bodily systems and processes including the way that genes, hormones and neurotransmitters affect our mind and behaviour

biological psychology – this area focuses on explaining thinking, emotion and cognition in terms of bodily systems, e.g. the nervous system and hormones

blind procedures – see *single blind* and *double blind*

BPS – British Psychological Society. An organisation in Britain responsible for producing a Code of Ethics and Ethical Guidelines to help psychologists to conduct their research ethically

C

capacity – the total amount of information that can be held in a memory store at one time, i.e. how much fits in before the store is full

cardiovascular diseases – illnesses relating to the heart and circulatory system (arteries, veins and capillaries). These include coronary heart disease and stroke

case study – an investigation of one person in detail using techniques such as interviewing, observation and conducting tests, which is often done on rare instances, such as children who have experienced privation that could not be created artificially but can provide useful information

catharsis – the discharge of emotion experienced when the energy associated with an unconscious memory is released

causal relationship – a relationship between two variables such that a change in one is responsible for a change in the other

ceiling effects – where the measure of a variable causes scores to cluster at the top of the range

central executive (CE) – an element of the working memory model which takes information in from the senses and sorts it before passing the right kinds of information to two slave units (the phonological loop and visuo-spatial sketch pad)

central tendency – see *measure of central tendency*

charismatic (or transformational) leadership – an explanation for obedience which suggests that effective authority figures have particular skills that encourage others to follow their orders. The specific personal characteristics they have and social processes they employ make them expert at influencing the beliefs, values, behaviour and performance of others

chronic – long-term (e.g. of stress)

chunk – a single unit of information which can be stored in STM

chunking – the combining of to-be-remembered items into meaningful units that can be stored in STM as a single unit i.e. a 'chunk'. This processes uses knowledge from LTM

citalopram – a selective serotonin reuptake inhibitor (a drug used to treat depression)

classical conditioning – the acquisition of new behaviours by association. A neutral stimulus is paired with an existing unconditioned stimulus which produces an unconditioned response. After repeated pairings the neutral stimulus becomes a conditioned stimulus capable of eliciting a conditioned response

closed questions – questions offering few alternative responses and no opportunity to expand on answers

code of ethics – a British Psychological Society (BPS) publication which identifies issues of respect, competence, responsibility and integrity for researchers that are important in their encounters with participants. The BPS also produces advisory guidelines for the conduct of psychological research in Britain

coding units – words or concepts identified in content analysis that are operationally defined and then counted to produce quantitative data

cognitive approach – an area of psychology which focuses on, and uses explanations (e.g. of abnormality) based on, the way an individual perceives and thinks

cognitive behaviour therapy (CBT) – a cognitive therapy used for people experiencing depression and the effects of stress. It aims to change faulty thinking by challenging dysfunctional beliefs and setting behavioural tasks to overcome irrational thinking, thus reducing symptoms

cognitive dissonance – the unpleasant feelings of arousal and anxiety we experience when we try to hold in mind two ideas that conflict. These feelings are reduced by changing our attitude (e.g. by accepting the beliefs of others) so is an explanation for conformity

cognitive interview – a technique used to improve accuracy for testimonies gained from witnesses which aims to recreate internal and environmental cues for the witness, to get them to report information in different orders and from different perspectives, and to report incomplete or irrelevant details

cognitive psychology – focuses on receiving, changing, storing and using information. It includes the processes of attention, perception, memory, decision-making and language

cognitive triad – an individual's related views about the self, the world and the future

cognitive vulnerability – thinking patterns which put an individual at risk of anxiety and depression

collaborative research – uses feedback from participants to identify important themes in qualitative data from interviews and case studies

compliance – changing our behaviour to go along with the majority without agreeing with them, or changing our minds about how we would like to act

compliant personality – an individual characteristic which is related to low independence, e.g. following majority behaviour or orders from an authority figure. Such individuals tend to be eager to please others and to avoid conflict

confidentiality – the ethical requirement for participants' individual results and personal information to be completely safe and private

conformity – a type of majority influence which occurs when a larger group of people influences a smaller number and individuals in the smaller group adjust their behaviour or opinions to fit in with the majority

consent – agreement from potential participants to provide sufficient information to understand what is being agreed to when they enter into psychological research. It must be independent of payment or the influence of a researcher's position of power

content analysis – a technique for investigating information in material such as magazines, television programmes and transcripts of interviews. Content such as specific words, ideas or feelings can be divided into categories or coding units. These may either be counted to produce quantitative data or described in detailed themes to produce qualitative data

context cue – an aspect of the external environment that is encoded with to-be-remembered information that can help with retrieval if it is present at recall, e.g. something we can see, hear or smell

contrived observation – see *controlled observation*

control – a way to standardise a procedure to avoid factors other than the IV affecting the DV so a cause-and-effect relationship can be established

control processes – features of the multi-store model that are functions rather than hypothetical structures. They include rehearsal to maintain items in STM and move them to LTM

controlled observation (contrived observation) – the participant is observed in a situation that has been set up by the researcher for the purpose of observing specific behaviours that have been decided in advance

conversion disorder – a condition in which negative emotions (e.g. stress) lead to a physical symptom with no physical basis, such as paralysis, deafness or blindness

coronary heart disease (CHD) – 'heart disease': a serious health problem which has symptoms such as high blood pressure and can lead to heart attacks

correlation – a relationship between two measured variables such that a change in one variable is related to a change in the other (although these changes may not be causal)

correlation coefficient – a mathematical measure of the extent to which a change in one variable is related to the change in another. The coefficient can vary from +1 (perfect positive correlation) to -1 (perfect negative correlation)

correlational analysis – research method used to investigate a link between two measured variables (co-variables)

corticotrophin-releasing hormone (CRH) – a hormone released by the hypothalamus in response to chronic stress, which causes the pituitary gland to release the adrenocorticotropic hormone

cortisol – a corticosteroid hormone released by the adrenal cortex in response to ACTH from the pituitary gland in situations of chronic stress. It makes more energy available through the breakdown of fats and release of glucose from the liver and reduces sympathetic activation and the release of adrenaline

counterbalancing – a way to overcome order effects in a repeated measures design. Each possible order of levels of the IV is performed by a different subgroup of participants. This can be described as an ABBA design as half the participants do condition A then B and half do B then A

critical period – a developmental stage during which an individual must have the opportunity to acquire a pattern of behaviour and after which it will be unable to do so

cross-cultural study – an investigation comparing variables such as attachment or mental health in people from two or more cultures

cue – a piece of information that is encoded at the same time as a to-be-remembered item that can later help with recall

culture – the set of behaviours and beliefs characterising a group of people such as a nationality

culture-bound – a concept, e.g. a theory or definition of abnormality, which only applies to the group in which it was developed, e.g. aspects of ideal mental health

D

day care – the provision of temporary daytime alternative care to parental care at home for pre-school children, e.g. with a childminder or in a nursery

debrief – a full explanation of the aims and potential consequences of research given to participants as soon as possible after completing a study and through which researchers can ensure that the participants' experiences were not distressing, and that they leave the study in at least as positive a mood as they entered it

deception – deliberately misinforming participants about the aims or procedures within an investigation

defence mechanisms – unconscious strategies such as denial that block unpleasant feelings and hence reduce moral strain

delayed recall – retrieving previously learned information following a delay (usually sufficiently long to cause decay from STM)

demand characteristics – aspects of an experimental setting that accidentally tell the participants the aim of the study. They can cause the participants' behaviour to change

denial – a psychological defence mechanism in which we refuse to admit an unpleasant fact to ourselves (such as that we are behaving in a morally objectionable way)

dependent personality disorder – a personality characterised by extreme dependence on and submission to others

dependent variable (DV) – the factor which the investigator measures in an experiment

depression – a mood disorder characterised by symptoms of dysphoria such as persistent sadness

deprivation – the temporary or permanent separation of a child from the primary carer(s) to whom they are attached

destructive obedience – following direct orders from an authority figure who tells us to do something immoral, such as harming or killing someone, which we do even if it distresses us

developmental psychology – an area of investigation focusing on how the human mind and behaviour change over the lifespan. As childhood is a time of rapid change, this is a key aspect

deviation from ideal mental health – a definition of abnormality which uses indicators of psychological well-being such as high self-esteem, personal growth, coping, being independent and having an accurate perception of reality

deviation from social norms – a definition of abnormality based on the individual exhibiting behaviour which differs from that of most members of their society and that is morally or socially unacceptable

Diagnostic and Statistical Manual of Mental Disorders (DSM) – a widely used tool for assessing and classifying mental disorders. It is produced by the American Psychiatric Association and is widely used in Britain. The current version (2000) is DSM-IV-TR

digit span – the maximum number of digits (numbers) we can keep in STM

directional hypothesis – a statement relating to the aim of an investigation which predicts how one variable will be related to another, e.g. in an experiment whether a change will produce an increase or a decrease in the DV or in a correlation whether an increase in one variable will be linked to an increase or a decrease in another variable

disclosed observation – watching and recording the behaviour of participants who are aware that they are being observed

disinhibited attachment – (Type D) a pattern of attachment behaviour typical of children who spend time in an institution

dispersion – see *measure of dispersion*

displacement – the expulsion of older items from STM when its limited capacity is reached as newer items enter

dizygotic twins (DZs) – non-identical twins formed by the fertilisation of two eggs at the same time (by different sperm) so that the two resulting embryos have different genes but develop in the uterus together. As they are full siblings they share 50 per cent of their genes on average. They can either be the same sex or different sexes

dopamine – a neurotransmitter (implicated in schizophrenia)

dose effect – the idea that long hours in day care have more of an effect than a few hours

double blind – an experimental procedure which protects against both demand characteristics and experimenter bias. It ensures that neither the researcher working with the participants nor the participants themselves are aware of which condition an individual is in

drug – a chemical molecule that affects the action of neurons so can change our emotions, cognitions or behaviour. They often act in the synaptic cleft, mimicking neurotransmitters, blocking receptors or preventing neurotransmitters from being removed from the synaptic cleft

DSM – see *Diagnostic and Statistical Manual of Mental Disorder*

duration – how long a memory is stored for, i.e. the length of storage of information over time

E

echoic – relating to sound

echoic store – the short-term sensory store or 'sensory memory' for sound-based information coming into the memory system through the ears

ecological validity – the extent to which findings generalise to other situations. This is affected by whether the situation (e.g. a lab) is a fair representation of the real world and whether the task is relevant (see *mundane realism*)

electroconvulsive therapy (ECT) – a biological therapy for depression using a small, short electric shock to the brain which causes a brief seizure

emotion-focused (EF) coping – a way of dealing with a stressor by reducing its negative effects so the individual feels better about the situation, e.g. ignoring the problem or moaning about it

encoding – the form of representation that is used to hold information in memory, e.g. visual (sight-based), acoustic (sound-based) or semantic (meaning-based)

endocrine gland – a body area which releases chemicals called hormones into the bloodstream. These target other parts of the body and change their activity

episodic buffer – a limited-capacity slave unit in the working memory model which allows the central executive to access LTM and transfer information back and forth between here and the phonological loop and visuo-spatial sketch pad

ethical guidelines – advice published by organisations such as the British Psychological Society (BPS), which helps psychologists to conduct research with human participants and therapy with clients in acceptable ways

ethical issues – factors that researchers should consider in the fair and reasonable treatment of participants, including respect, competence, responsibility and integrity (see also *code of ethics*)

evolution – the process by which individuals with adaptive behaviours are selected by factors in the environment that cause better rates of survival and reproduction so their behaviours are passed on to subsequent generations and become more common in the population

experiment – a study in which an IV is manipulated and consequent changes in a DV are measured in order to establish a causes and effect relationship

experimental design – the way in which participation in an experiment is organised. Participants can perform in only one or all of the levels of the IV. This may be repeated measures, independent groups or matched pairs

experimenter bias – the effect of an experimenter's expectations on the results of a study, e.g. caused by differences in the way an experimenter behaves towards participants in different conditions

external locus of control – the belief that one is unable to determine events in one's own life, i.e. that events just happen to us (so is associated with high conformity)

extraneous variable – a factor that could affect the DV and hide the effect of the IV in an experiment, so threaten validity

F

failure to function adequately – a definition of abnormality based on an individual's capacity to deal with everyday tasks such as washing, socialising or working

Fascism (F) Scale – a test of authoritarianism on which people with authoritarian personalities gain high scores

fatigue effect – a decrease in performance on a task due to repetition, e.g. because of boredom or tiredness

field experiment – a study in which the researcher manipulates an IV and measures a DV in the natural setting of the participants

filler questions – questions included in a questionnaire to disguise the aim and reduce demand characteristics

flooding – a behavioural therapy in which patients are exposed to an extreme form of the thing they fear

floor effects – where the measure of a variable causes scores to cluster at the bottom of the range

focused observations – an observational technique in which specific, operationally defined behavioural categories are recorded from the stream of behaviour

free association – a technique used in psychoanalysis to reveal unconscious thoughts by encouraging the patient to describe things as they come into their head, e.g. in response to a question or word. These responses are then interpreted by the analyst

free recall – the accessing of stored memories without, or with minimal, prompts

G

GAF – see *Global Assessment of Functioning*

generalisability – the extent to which findings gained in one context (e.g. setting or group of people) can be applied to another context in order to understand or explain behaviour, cognition or emotions (i.e. working from a specific situation to a general one)

genotype – the total genetic make-up of an individual

Global Assessment of Functioning (GAF) – a rating scale used to assign a score from 1 to 100 to indicate how well a person is coping

H

Hassles Scale – a list of 117 negative things that could annoy people on a daily basis (e.g. losing things or having too much to do). The total score on the scale is linked to symptoms of stress

histogram – a graph used to illustrate continuous data, e.g. to show the distribution of a set of scores

hypothalamus – a small, complex part of the brain which interacts with both the nervous system and the endocrine system

hypothesis – a testable statement which predicts a relationship between variables such as in an experiment where one change will produce an increase or a decrease in the DV, or in a correlation where an increase in one variable will be linked to an increase or a decrease in another variable

I

I-can't-stand-it-itis – the belief that when something does not go smoothly it is a disaster, which makes us overreact to minor problems

iconic – relating to visual (or 'pictorial') information

iconic store – the short-term sensory store or 'sensory memory' for visual information coming into the memory system through the eyes

ideal mental health – criteria such as having high self-esteem, being independent and perceiving reality accurately which, in their absence, are used to judge abnormality in the way that the absence of a normal body temperature can be used to judge abnormal physical health

identical twins – see *monozygotic twins*

identification – changing behaviour or beliefs in order to become like an individual or group that is admired (so can explain conformity, especially in relation to behaviours)

immediate recall – retrieving previously learned information without a delay (allowing access to items in STM)

immune system – the body structures and mechanisms used to fight disease, including lymphocytes

impersonal memories – an individual's store of information about events not directly connected to themselves

imprinting – the attachment (and following behaviour) of newly hatched chicks (and some other species) to the first moving object they see after hatching or birth. It allows them to learn about food and future mates, and keeps them safe

incidental learning – when memories are formed without any deliberate effort by the learner

independence – the behaviour of an individual who chooses not to conform to the majority or to obey an order from an authority figure, i.e. who resists social influence

independent groups design – an experimental design in which different groups of participants are used for each level of the IV

independent variable (IV) – the factor which the investigator manipulates in an experiment

individual differences – variation between people, e.g. in terms of their behaviour, cognitions or emotions (which could lead to differences in their responses in experiments that are not caused by the IV). They may be genetic or acquired in origin

informational social influence – the effect of a majority which causes us to conform because we believe they are right, e.g. because they are better informed than us or when the situation is ambiguous, so both our private beliefs and public behaviour change

informed consent – an issue in investigations using human participants is whether they have received sufficient information to make a reasoned decision about whether they want to participate. BPS guidelines suggest that potential participants should be given enough detail about the study to be able to decide, i.e. to give their informed consent

instinct – an inborn tendency to behave in a particular way

institutionalisation – the consequences for a child's attachment and behaviour when they spend much of their time being cared for away from the home, such as in an orphanage

inter-observability – the extent to which two or more researchers who watch the same sequence of behaviour will produce identical records of the events

interactional synchrony – the linked responses of mother and baby pairs during which they take turns and imitate each other's movements

interference – additional information which disrupts memory processes. It can affect either encoding or retrieval and reduces the accuracy of memory

internal locus of control – the belief that one is able to determine events in one's own life (so is associated with low conformity)

internal working model – a mental representation of how relationships work based on a child's first attachment, which determines adult relationships such as their own later parenting behaviour

internalisation – changing our behaviour to go along with majority behaviour because we have been convinced that they are correct so our beliefs have changed, i.e. altering our private attitudes and public behaviour to mirror those of a group

interval data – a level of measurement which records data as points on a scale which has equal gaps between the points but does not have a real zero, e.g. standardised measures such as IQ tests

interview – a self-report research method in which participants reply verbally to questions typically asked face-to-face

investigator effects – any unwitting influence a researcher has on the participants. These include experimenter bias and the effects of researchers in non-experimental investigations such as in interviews or observations

ironic deviance – the reduction in likelihood of conforming to a group norm which appears not to be independent behaviour. So, when an attribution of conformity or obedience is made to explain the behaviour of a group, they will lack informational social influence

K

killer T cells – cells within the immune system; they are a special type of lymphocyte responsible for removing cancerous cells

L

laboratory experiment – a study conducted in an artificial, controlled environment in which the experimenter manipulates an IV and measures the consequent changes in a DV whilst controlling extraneous variables

learning theory – a term covering theories explaining how new behaviours are acquired, including through classical conditioning and operant conditioning

levels of measurement – the type of quantitative data obtained (see *nominal, ordinal, interval* and *ratio data*)

life changes – events that require readjustment in lifestyle so cause stress and affect health. A value of 'Life Change Units' depends on how traumatic the event feels; very negative ones, such as the death of a spouse, have high stress scores but even positive changes, e.g. Christmas, can contribute. The total stress score over a given time is measured on the SRRS

Likert scales – a closed question type used in questionnaires which consists of a statement followed by opinion choices, e.g. strongly agree, agree, don't know, disagree, strongly disagree

locus of control – the beliefs an individual has about the cause of events in their lives, which may be internal (self-determined) or external (governed by factors beyond the individual's sphere of influence). Rotter (1966) suggests this can account for conformity because an external locus of control makes people accepting of the influence of others

long-term memory (LTM) – a memory store in the multi-store model which has a vast capacity, a long duration and encodes information semantically

longitudinal study – one in which the same people are followed up over long periods to investigate their development

lymphocyte – a type of white blood cell that defends the body against disease. Some fight infection, others target cancerous cells

M

major depression – a serious mood disorder in which symptoms of dysphoria are extreme but intermittent as opposed to the milder but constant minor depression

matched pairs design – an experimental design in which participants are arranged into pairs. Each pair is similar in ways that are important to the study and the members of each pair perform in the two different levels of the IV

maternal sensitivity hypothesis – the idea that the attachment type of the child depends on the behaviour of the main carer, e.g. their level of sensitive responsiveness

mean – a measure of central tendency worked out by adding up all the scores and dividing by the number of scores

measure of central tendency – a mathematical way to describe a typical or average score from a data set (such as using the mode, median or mean)

measure of dispersion – a mathematical way to describe how spread out the scores in a data set are (such as the range or standard deviation)

median – a measure of central tendency worked out as the middle score in the list when the data are in rank order (from smallest to largest). If there are two numbers in the middle they are added together and divided by two

memory – the encoding and storage of information that is later retrieved

method of loci – a strategy for improving memory that uses a familiar route to cue the recall of newly learned information

minority influence – the effect of a small number of people (or single individual) who change the beliefs, and therefore behaviour, of the majority. To be most effective, minorities need to be committed, flexible, consistent and have a clear, relevant message

MMPI (Minnesota Multiphasic Personality Inventory) – a general personality test

mnemonic – a memory aid, such as a semantic or visual cue that can help with recall, e.g. by organising the to-be-remembered information so that it is easy to retrieve

modality specific – a feature of memory stores such as the short-term sensory store or 'sensory memory' where incoming information is coded in the same form as it enters, e.g. acoustic information is represented using a sound-based code

mode – a measure of central tendency worked out as the most frequent score(s) in a set of results

monoamine oxidase inhibitors (MAOIs) – drugs for depression which reduce the rate at which monoamine neurotransmitters are broken down so that levels build up

monotropy – the tendency of infants to instinctively form a single, unique attachment to the mother (or main carer) during a critical period early in life which affects future relationships

monozygotic twins (MZs) – identical twins formed by the splitting of a single fertilised egg so that the two resulting embryos are genetically exactly the same, i.e. they share 100 per cent of their genes. They are therefore always the same sex

mood stabilisers – drugs used to treat bipolar disorder (manic depression)

moral strain – the unpleasant sensation of feeling obliged to follow an order that violates our own moral code. These feelings can be reduced by defence mechanisms such as denial

multi-store model (MSM) – a theory of memory proposing three memory stores (the STSS, STM and LTM) and control processes such as rehearsal

mundane realism – the similarity of an experimental task to normal activities. Where tasks are like those performed in day-to-day life, mundane realism is high

musturbation – the tendency to think that we must succeed in everything, which makes us very sensitive to failure

N

natural experiment – a study in which an experimenter makes use of an existing change or difference in situations to create levels of an IV and then measures the DV in each condition

naturalistic observation – the participant is watched in their own environment, i.e. in the normal place for the activity being observed

negative automatic thinking – dysfunctional cognitive processing associated with depression in which the individual holds negative views about their self, the world and the future, which feed back and reinforce one another

negative correlation – a relationship between two variables where an increase in one accompanies a decrease in the other. The correlation coefficient will be a negative number

negative feedback – a control process in which increasing activation reduces the trigger for activation so it is self-terminating (e.g. the effect of cortisol in the blood on the hypothalamus is such that less CRH is produced so less cortisol is released)

negative self-schema – see *self-schema*

neuroleptic malignant syndrome – a rare complication of antipsychotic drugs which causes neurological damage and can lead to permanent brain damage or death

neuroleptics – see *antipsychotics*

neuron – a cell in the nervous system which communicates messages using electrical signals along its length and chemical signals (neurotransmitters) at the gaps between cells (synaptic cleft)

neurotransmitter – a molecule released by a neuron which transmits a message from one neuron to the next. The molecules attach to special receptor sites on the membrane of the next neuron. There are many different neurotransmitters, e.g. serotonin, dopamine and noradrenaline

nominal data – a level of measurement which records data as totals in named categories such as the number of infants who are attachment Types A, B, C or D or the number of participants saying 'yes' or 'no'

non-directional hypothesis – a statement relating to the aim of an investigation which predicts how one variable will be related to another, e.g. whether there will be a difference in the DV between levels of the IV (in an experiment) or that there will be a relationship between the measured variables (in a correlation)

non-disclosed observation – watching and recording the behaviour of participants who are unaware that they are being observed

non-focused observation – the recording of any relevant behaviours which are exhibited during an episode of study

non-identical twins – see *dizygotic twins*

non-participant observation – the observer is hidden from the participant(s) being observed, e.g. by using a video camera

noradrenaline – a neurotransmitter that is released from the adrenal medulla into the bloodstream like a hormone in response to stress, which helps to maintain sympathetic activation. (It is also implicated in depression)

noradrenaline reuptake inhibitors (NRIs) – drugs which block the recycling of noradrenaline so increase the level of this neurotransmitter in the synaptic gap. They are used to treat depression

normative social influence – the effect of a majority which causes us to conform because we want to be liked or accepted or to avoid rejection, so our public behaviour changes but our private beliefs do not

O

obedience – following direct orders from a person in a position of authority over us

objectivity – taking an external perspective that is not affected by an individual or personal viewpoint

observation – a research method in which data collection is achieved by watching and recording the activity of people (or animals). This may be done in an artificial setting (contrived or controlled observations) or in the participants' normal environment

obsessive-compulsive disorder (OCD) – an anxiety disorder in which patients show repetitive thoughts or behaviours such as compulsive washing

open questions – questions allowing participants to give full and detailed answers in their own words

operant conditioning – a process by which behavioural changes occur when actions are reinforced (which increases the frequency of the behaviour) or punished (which decreases the frequency of the behaviour)

operational definition – see *operationalisation*

operationalisation – defining variables so they can be accurately manipulated, measured and replicated

opportunity sampling – selecting participants according to availability. It is non-representative

oral stage – first stage of Freud's psychosexual theory of development (0–1 year) during which a child's focus is on its mouth

order effects – changes in participants' performance due to repeating the same or similar test more than once. They can confuse the effect of the IV on the DV in a repeated measures design

ordinal data – a level of measurement which records data as points along a scale, such as a rating or Likert scale such that the points fall in order, but there are not necessarily equal gaps between those points

P

paraphilia – a sexual disorder in which the patient becomes sexually aroused in response to non-sexual stimuli

parasympathetic nervous system (pANS) – the part of the ANS activated during relaxation that produces changes such as decreased heart rate. It calms us down when a stressor subsides

participant observation – the observer is a member of the group or activity being observed

participant variables – individual differences between participants (such as age, skills, personality) that could affect their responses in a study

peg-word system – a strategy for improving memory that uses a rhyme to cue the recall of newly learned information

permastore – a store of very long-term memories

personal memories – an individual's store of information that relates to their own life

personality – the aspects of a person that make their behaviour consistent and distinct from that of other people, e.g. in terms of the ability to resist conforming and obeying

phenotype – an individual's physical and psychological characteristics. It is the product of both genotype and environment

phobia – an irrational fear of an object or situation

phonological loop (PL) – a slave unit in the working memory model which holds sound-based items (including speech), uses an acoustic code and has a duration of 2–3 seconds (which can be increased with rehearsal), i.e. is time-limited

pilot study – a small-scale trial run of a method to identify any practical problems and resolve them

pituitary-adrenal system (PAS) – the link between the pituitary and adrenal glands which is responsible for the control of the long-term response to stress, e.g. having a stressful job or living in a crowded place

placebo – a substitute for a real treatment that is given as a control condition in a study of medical or psychological treatment. In drug studies this is an inactive chemical

population – all of the people within a given group (e.g. geographical area, religion or school) who could, potentially, be selected in the sample

positive correlation – a relationship between two variables where an increase in one accompanies an increase in the other. The correlation coefficient will be a positive number

positive feedback – a control process in which increasing activation increases the trigger for activation so it is self-perpetuating (e.g. the effect of adrenaline and noradrenaline and the sANS)

practice effect – improvement in performance on a task due to repetition, e.g. because of familiarity with or memory of the task

presumptive consent – gaining agreement to participate in principle from a similar group of people to the intended participants by asking them if they would object to the procedure. It can be used when gaining informed consent from the participants themselves would lead to them working out the aim of the study

primacy effect – the tendency to recall the earliest items in a list very well (better than those in the middle of the list). It arises because these items have been passed into LTM

privacy – an ethical issue relating to avoiding the invasion of emotions or physical space. It is an invasion of privacy to observe participants in locations where they would expect to be unseen

privation – the failure of an infant to form an attachment, e.g. when they are severely neglected or abused

problem-focused (PF) coping – a way of dealing with stress by reducing or removing the stressor, e.g. taking practical steps using advice or past experience

protection from harm – the ethical requirement that participants should not be likely to suffer physical and psychological harm from participation and that they will not experience any greater risk than they would expect in their usual lifestyle

proximity seeking – staying close to an attachment figure

psychoanalysis – a 'talking cure' devised by Freud as a therapy for patients with psychological problems that did not appear to be biological in origin. Important processes in analysis are free association, catharsis, transference and reparenting. The analyst provides the patient with an interpretation of their current problems in relation to their childhood traumas, early relationships and unconscious processes

psychodynamic approach – an area of psychology which focuses on, and uses explanations (e.g. of abnormality) based on the idea that early relationships, traumatic childhood experiences and unconscious processes affect our thinking and behaviour

Q

qualitative data – descriptive data providing depth and detail

quantitative data – numerical data collected as totals in named categories or on numerical scales (see also *levels of measurement*)

questionnaire – a self-report method using written questions

R

random allocation – the dividing of participants in an independent groups design into the levels of the IV in a way that ensures each individual has an equal chance of ending up in any condition

random control trial – a procedure in which any patient has an equal chance of being allocated to a treatment or control condition. The outcomes are compared

random sampling – selecting participants such that each member of a population has an equal chance of being chosen. It is representative of the population

randomisation – a procedure used in a repeated measures design to counteract order effects by ensuring that each participant has an equal chance of performing the levels of the IV in any order

range – a measure of spread calculated as the difference between the smallest and the largest score in a data set

ratio data – a level of measurement which records data as points on a scale which has equal gaps between the points and a real zero, e.g. centimetres or beats-per-minute

rational emotive behaviour therapy (REBT) – a cognitive therapy used for people experiencing depression and the effects of stress. It confronts apparently irrational beliefs with the aim of disrupting them and causing changes which may be *cognitive* (changing beliefs to rational ones), *emotional* (changing negative feelings to positive ones) or *behavioural* (changing behaviour to improve coping)

raw data – the original scores obtained from all the participants in a study

reactance – the rebellious behaviour which arises as a consequence of the anger we experience when our freedom of choice is deliberately restricted (so is an explanation for independent behaviour)

recency effect – the tendency to recall the last few items in a list very well (better than those in the middle of the list). It arises because these items still remain in STM when recalled

recognition – the accessing of memories by identifying things which have been encountered before

reconstructive memory – the idea that remembered information is not recorded perfectly but that memories are 'rebuilt' when they are retrieved so can be affected by additional 'post event' information

rehearsal – the non-verbal repetition of items in STM. It can both extend the duration of STM (maintenance rehearsal) and transfer items to LTM

reliability – the consistency of a measure, e.g. whether results from the same participants would be similar each time

reparenting – the experience in psychoanalysis of having a good-quality relationship with a responsible adult

repeated measures design – an experimental design in which each participant performs in every level of the IV

replication – repeating an investigation in an identical way to an original procedure. If replication produces similar results, this indicates good reliability

representative – a feature of a sample which is typical of the key features of a population so is likely to produce findings which can be generalised

repression – an unconscious defence mechanism that protects us from unpleasant memories so causes us to be unable to retrieve traumatic events

resistance – an individual's capacity to avoid conforming or obeying when the situation demands these behaviours

resistant attachment – (Type C) an insecure attachment type where children intensely seek proximity, become very distressed in the carer's absence and in the presence of a stranger but display a negative reuniting response

retrieval – the accessing of information held in memory

retrospective consent – gaining agreement to use results that have already been gained from participants who were previously unaware that they were part of a study

reuniting response – the behaviour displayed by an infant towards the reappearance of their primary carer after a period of absence

right to withdraw – an ethical issue which obliges the researcher to inform participants that they can leave a study at any time (regardless of payment) and take their data with them. It may also be important to remind them of this right

S

sample – the group of people selected from a population to represent that population in a study

sampling technique – the way in which the group of participants (the sample) is selected from the population

scattergram – a graph used to display the data from a correlational study. Each point represents the participant's score on scales for each of the two measured variables

schizophrenia – a serious mental disorder with symptoms such as hallucinations, irrational beliefs and a distorted perception of reality

secure attachment – (Type B) the most common attachment type where children play independently but seek proximity, show secure base behaviour, become moderately distressed in the carer's absence and in the presence of a stranger and display a positive reuniting response

secure base behaviour – regularly returning to an attachment figure when exploring

selective noradrenaline reuptake inhibitors (SNRIs) – see *noradrenaline reuptake inhibitors*

selective serotonin reuptake inhibitors (SSRIs) – drugs for depression (e.g. Prozac, Seroxat and citalopram) that reduce the rate at which the neurotransmitter serotonin is recycled so increase the amount available in the synaptic gap to stimulate receptors. They may also be used to treat the symptoms of stress

self-report methods – ways to obtain data by asking participants to provide information about themselves, e.g. interviews and questionnaires

self-schema – a cognitive framework containing all our information about ourselves, e.g. our beliefs and feelings, that is used to interpret new information about ourselves. When we are exposed to criticism in childhood these may become negative

semantic – relating to meaning. For example LTM uses a semantic code, i.e. the items are stored using a meaning-based code

semi-structured interview – a self-report technique in which some questions are fixed but others can be added, offering a compromise between being standardised and gaining detail

sensitive period – an age at which a child is much more likely to develop a pattern of behaviour if particular conditions occur

sensitive responsiveness – the ability of the primary carer to notice and respond appropriately to signals from the baby

sensory memory – see *short-term sensory store*

separation – long- or short-term deprivation (see *deprivation*)

separation distress – the anxiety caused by being apart from an attachment figure

serial position task – a test of memory requiring participants to remember a list of items (e.g. words). The frequency of items recalled from the beginning, middle and end of the list is recorded. It is used to illustrate the difference between STM and LTM (see also *primacy effect* and *recency effect*)

serotonin – a neurotransmitter (implicated in depression)

short-term memory (STM) – a memory store in the multi-store model which has a limited capacity (7±2 chunks), a short duration (less than 30 seconds) and encodes information acoustically

short-term sensory store (STSS) – a store in the multi-store model which has a moderate capacity, a very limited duration and which encodes information using modality-specific representation. Sometimes called 'sensory memory'

single blind – an experimental procedure which ensures that the participants are unaware of the level of the IV in which they are performing. This helps to reduce the effect of demand characteristics

SNRIs – see *selective noradrenaline reuptake inhibitors*

social control – strategies that are used to deliberately influence the behaviour of particular groups in a society (such as diagnosing people with mental illnesses in order to restrict their freedom)

social desirability bias – the tendency of participants to answer questions in ways that reflect what they think is acceptable in society rather than what they necessarily believe

social influence – the effect that one or more individuals have on other individuals, e.g. through conformity and obedience

social norm – a belief or behaviour that the majority of people within a society hold or do

social psychology – the branch of psychology which focuses on how people interact and affect one another

social readjustment rating scale (SRRS) – a questionnaire of life events, each of which has a stress score that can be added up to give a single score. This indicates the stress experienced and is linked to ill health (the higher the stress score, the greater the risk of illness)

social releasers – babies' behaviours, such as smiling and cooing, which elicit care from adults

SSRIs – see *selective serotonin reuptake inhibitors*

stability – the extent to which a child keeps to the same day care arrangements

standard deviation – a measure of spread calculated as the average variation either side of the mean

standardised instructions – a set of written or spoken guidelines for experimenters to inform participants about what they are expected to do. They help to reduce variation between participants and between levels of the IV so improve validity and reliability

standardised procedures – the use of controls to ensure that an experimental test is performed in the same way each time to improve reliability

state cue – an internal factor such as an emotion or physiological condition that is present during learning so is encoded with to-be-remembered information that can help with retrieval if it is the same at recall, e.g. feeling scared or sad

stimulants – drugs which increase the level of activity in the nervous system. Some are used to treat attention deficit disorders and narcolepsy

stranger anxiety – distress in the presence of an unfamiliar person

stress – our biological and psychological responses to threats we feel we cannot overcome

stress management – the use of external strategies to reduce the impact of stressors. These include cognitive behavioural therapy, rational emotive behaviour therapy, drugs and biofeedback

stressor – internal or external sources of threat which we feel are beyond our capacity to control or avoid

structured interview – a self-report technique in which all questions are fixed so the procedure for every participant is standardised

sympathetic nervous system (sANS) – the part of the ANS activated during arousal that produces changes such as increased heart rate. It triggers the initial response to an acute stressor

sympathomedullary pathway (SMP) – the system that responds to acute stressors consisting of the sANS and adrenaline

synapse – the working unit of pre- and post-synaptic membranes and synaptic cleft which is the site of communication between neurons by neurotransmitters (and is the site of action for many drugs)

synaptic cleft – the gap between neurons across which neurotransmitters transmit messages (and at which many drugs act)

systematic desensitisation (SD) – a therapy based on the behavioural approach, which uses classical conditioning. Patients (e.g. with phobias) are exposed step-by-step to an anxiety hierarchy of more frightening stimuli whilst a relaxed state is maintained by the therapist. Through this they unlearn the association between the object or situation and fear

T

talking cure – therapies which use discussion between a patient/client and a therapist to resolve psychological problems. Freud's psychoanalysis was the first of these and has led to present-day counselling

tardive dyskinesia – a side effect of some antipsychotic drugs which results from neurological damage, which produces uncontrollable limb and facial movements

target population – the group from which a sample is drawn

technophobia – a fear of computers and/or related technology

thematic analysis – a method for extracting and representing qualitative data from sources such as interviews and content analyses. Key concepts (which may be repeated or infrequent but important) are identified in advance and illustrated with examples

themes – coding units from content analysis which are combined into pre-existing or emergent categories to represent key ideas in the qualitative data

transference – the playing out of an individual's relationships with key people in their lives, such as parents, in their behaviour towards a psychoanalyst

transformational leadership – see *charismatic leadership*

transition – the process where a child used to full-time care at home is introduced to day care

tricyclics – a group of drugs for depression

true experiment – a research method in which the experimenter has control over the IV so sets up conditions and randomly allocates participants to levels of the IV, e.g. laboratory and field experiments

twin studies – a technique used to attempt to separate the effects of genes and family environment. Comparisons may be made between identical twins (MZs) reared together and reared apart, or to assess the relative similarity between identical and non-identical (DZ) twins

Type A attachment – see *avoidant attachment*

Type A personality – a trait typified by competitiveness, aggression and goal-directed behaviour, e.g. always in a hurry, enjoys high-risk sports, has a high-powered job, and so on. It is associated with high stress levels and ill health (e.g. a greater risk of CHD)

Type B attachment – see *secure attachment*

Type B personality – a trait typified by a relaxed attitude to life. Type Bs are less competitive and aggressive. They experience less stress and suffer less CHD

Type C attachment – see *resistant attachment*

Type C personality – a trait typified by repressed emotions and self-doubt. Such individuals tend to have little social support so they experience stress and suffer ill health

Type D attachment – see *disinhibited attachment*

Type D personality – a trait typified by anxiety, distress and pessimism. Such individuals experience stress and suffer ill health

U

unilateral – one side, e.g. an electric shock given to only one side of the head in ECT

unstructured interview – a technique which generally begins with the same question, but from there, questions depend on the respondent's answers

Uplifts Scale – a list of 135 positive things (e.g. getting things done or feeling healthy). Uplifts only relate to health inasmuch as they reduce the impact of hassles – if we have hassles we experience stress but if we have uplifts as well they help us to cope

V

validity – the extent to which a test measures what it set out to measure (see also *ecological validity*)

virtual reality – a three-dimensional computer simulation in which participants wearing special helmets perceive themselves to be inside the environment

visuo-spatial sketch (or scratch) pad (VSSP) – a slave unit in the working memory model which holds visual and spatial information

volunteer sampling – a way to recruit people through advertising; the participants respond to a request rather than being approached by the experimenter. It is non-representative

W

withdrawal – see *right to withdraw*

work stress – specific aspects of a job that make it more difficult to cope with

working memory model – a theory explaining the encoding, storage and retrieval of information which elaborates on the simple view of the short-term memory. It proposes four subunits, the central executive, the phonological loop, the visuo-spatial sketch pad and the episodic buffer

Y

Yerkes-Dodson Law (Inverted U Law) – the tendency to recall best when the level of arousal is moderate and worse when it is very high or low

notes

notes

notes

notes